Chaplaincy: Being God's Presence in Closed Communities

A Free Methodist History 1935-2010

E. Dean Cook

authorHOUSE®

AuthorHouse™
1663 Liberty Drive
Bloomington, IN 47403
www.authorhouse.com
Phone: 1-800-839-8640

©*2010 E. Dean Cook. All rights reserved.*

No part of this book may be reproduced, stored in a retrieval system, or transmitted by any means without the written permission of the author.

First published by AuthorHouse   5/19/2010

ISBN: 978-1-4490-8302-1 (e)
ISBN: 978-1-4490-8301-4 (sc)
ISBN: 978-1-4520-2610-7 (hc)

Library of Congress Control Number: 2010901874

Printed in the United States of America
Bloomington, Indiana

This book is printed on acid-free paper.

Free Methodist Chaplains Association
Copyright 2010

Table of Contents

Chapter One: Definition and Biblical Foundation of the Chaplaincy — 1

Chapter Two: Chaplain as a Person and Representative of the Church — 5

Chapter Three: Development of the Free Methodist Chaplaincy — 9

Chapter Four: Military Chaplaincy — 19

Chapter Five: Hospital Chaplaincy — 67

Chapter Six: Veterans Administration Chaplaincy — 81

Chapter Seven: Hospice Chaplaincy — 93

Chapter Eight: Correctional Facility Chaplaincy — 107

Chapter Nine: Retirement Community Chaplaincy — 123

Chapter Ten: Civil Air Patrol Chaplaincy — 135

Chapter Eleven: Police and Firefighters Chaplaincy — 143

Chapter Twelve: Campus Chaplaincy — 153

Conclusion — 163

Appendixes — 165
    A. Seeking A Chaplain Position
    B. Listing of Endorsing Agents
    C. Listing of Chaplain Association Presidents
    D. Listing of Chaplains
    E. Listing of Chaplain Professional Organizations

Selected Bibliography — 183

PREFACE

THIS IS THE FIRST ATTEMPT to set forth the history of the ministry of the Free Methodist Church chaplaincy. Numerous efforts have been made in the past to collect chaplain historical artifacts, oral histories and written accounts of individual chaplains, but this is the first comprehensive effort to put it all together in book form.

The purpose of this writing is, first, to preserve the rich history of our chaplaincy and to highlight some of the unique personalities who represent all chaplains. Secondly, it is our aim to honor Christ who called this ministry to closed communities into existence. Thirdly, it is our intent to inform and inspire the Church to recognize chaplaincy as a calling and to provide prayer support. Finally, we hope this work will make a significant contribution to our Church's historical record and that it would inspire further interest and research into this rich area of study.

The accounts recorded here were gleaned from the Marston Historical Center, the files of the Free Methodist Endorsing Office and Chaplains Association records, Church publications, Ministry Center records, letters, reports, writings and personal interviews. Future chapters await another writer as Free Methodist chaplains continue to venture out into new areas such as sports, camps, industry, and beyond. The words of Christ compel us to go: *"Here I am! I stand at the door and knock. If anyone hears my voice and opens the door, I will come in and eat with him, and he with me."* (Revelation 3:20 NIV)

It is with great affection
that we dedicate this book to
Chaplain Harry "Bud" and Lois Ansted;
Air Force Colonel, missionaries to Africa, Endorsing Agent/ Director
of Chaplains, Chaplains Association Executive Committee.

For over half a century, you have given dedicated service to the Church and its Chaplains through your leadership, example, and inspiration. Your lives and work, on behalf of chaplains, continue to advance this vital ministry in the Church and in the closed communities where chaplains serve.

Thank you sincerely
for your dedicated service.

Chaplain Rex Carpenter with wife, Louise
Endorsing Agent/Director of Chaplains

Chaplain Sam Shreffler
President of Chaplains Association

INTRODUCTION

CHAPLAINS HAVE SERVED THE CHURCH faithfully and tirelessly in war and in peace, in prisons, and hospitals, on battlefields and on campuses, with law enforcement officers and firemen, in rest homes and communities of seniors, with Hospice and the Civil Air Patrol - the settings grow almost annually. These are our ministers beyond the church doors. They all have one thing in common: they minister to closed communities.

By closed communities we mean that local clergy do not have the freedom to enter these settings as they might enter the communities that surround their church. When we say "closed" we do not imply that all have the same degree of nonadmission. For example, a military base is surrounded by a wire fence with guards on the gates. No one is given entrance unless they have special reason to be there and then their movement is restricted. Correctional Facilities exercise even greater restriction. Clergy cannot simply go to a jail or prison and expect entrance to see whomever they please. Hospitals ask that all clergy sign in and while in the hospital their ministry can be monitored to make sure the patient's rights and wishes are respected. These settings all vary in degree of restrictions but their mission requires that they limit access to their communities. The chaplaincy, however, is an accepted means by which the church can gain access to these institutions and for the communities to enjoy the rich ministry offered by clergy. Thus our title, "Ministry to Closed Communities: A Free Methodist History."

Since this special ministry takes place beyond the structure and eyes of the Church, little is written about it in church publications. Chaplains, out of respect for confidentiality and the institutions they serve, traditionally have not written a great deal about their work except in professional magazines. All of this has led to a serious gap in the Church's understanding and awareness of this ministry.

In view of this, at the 2008 Free Methodist Chaplains Professional Conference conducted at Cannon Beach, Oregon, the Chaplains Association Executive Committee voted to authorize preliminary work to begin on the research and writing of the Free Methodist Chaplaincy History. Chaplain Dean Cook, who had already been researching the history, was authorized to begin the work. Cook prepared a proposal which included a structure and time line for completing the project and submitted it to the President of the Association, the Director of Chaplains and the Executive Committee. The proposal was accepted and work began immediately at the Marston Historical Center in the World Ministry Center located in Indianapolis. Cathy Fortner, Director of the Center, opened the Archives fully for the required research and was invaluable in providing important material and guidance for the study. Equally valuable were the chaplains themselves who retain a large portion of this valuable history in their heads and offices. Without this assistance, this work would not have been possible. Chaplain Rex Carpenter, our Endorsing Agent/Director of Chaplains, provided invaluable help from his files and his own personal knowledge of our history.

The structure of the book begins with a discussion of the general history of chaplaincy ministry. Here special attention is given to the biblical basis for the chaplaincy, and to the chaplain as a person and representative of the church. The study then focuses on the major chaplain settings: Military, Hospitals, Veterans Administration, Hospice, Corrections, Senior Citizens, Law Enforcement and Firemen, Civil Air Patrol, and Campus ministries. The work then concludes with helpful guidance for those interested in pursuing the chaplaincy, a conclusion that touches on lessons learned from the research, and suggestions of areas for further study. Finally, an appendix is included with a number of useful listings and a limited bibliography.

We regret that time, space and resources do not allow for all our chaplains to receive equal treatment. Those highlighted are meant to be representative of all our fine chaplains.

CHAPTER ONE
DEFINITION OF AND BIBLICAL FOUNDATION FOR THE CHAPLAINCY

DEFINITION

AFTER RETIRING AS A CAREER military chaplain, I was appointed to one of the larger churches in our conference. One Sunday a visiting pastor shook my hand at the door and startled me by saying loud enough for those around us to hear "Isn't it interesting that they would assign a chaplain to pastor a church like this?" I wondered, what was his concept of a chaplain? Later, when I became a teacher and mentor to seminary students, one of my tasks was to help ministerial students think through their calling. It was my custom to ask if they had considered the chaplaincy as a calling. Invariably they would reply, "What is a chaplain and what do they do?" Their question reminded me that the chaplaincy remained, in some ways, the "mystery ministry" of the church. This inspired me to tell the chaplaincy story.

Saint Martin's Cloak

NO DEFINITION OF THE CHAPLAIN is complete without setting forth the story of Saint Martin. This fourth century French soldier was said to have encountered a beggar one day who was cold and without a coat. The soldier had compassion on the beggar, cut his own cloak in two, and gave him half for warmth. Later it was revealed to Martin through a dream or vision, that the beggar was actually Christ. The story goes that miraculously the cloak was restored whole and Martin was inspired to leave the army and become a priest for Christ. His cloak, called a "capella" in Latin, later became a sacred relic which French kings carried into battle to insure victory. The priest assigned to keep the cloak was called a "cappellanus" or chaplain. The place of worship for the chaplain and his flock was called a "chapel." Later there developed also a style of print, like a church text, but much more ornate, called a "chapel text". The office of chaplain came to be called the chaplaincy. The roles and meaning of chaplains have greatly expanded over the centuries and their numbers have grown rapidly in the past half-century. Today, chaplains still provide a vital ministry to closed communities beyond the church doors, wherever people are found.

Chaplains are normally ordained and are officially endorsed clergy of some recognized religious body; however, some people do function as volunteer chaplains without ordination and/or endorsement. The chaplain ministry has grown rapidly over the last fifty years as both the Church and institutional settings have recognized the great need for such a ministry model and have worked to develop a mutually acceptable relationship between the institution and religious ministry.

A Ministry to All

PERHAPS THE MOST UNIQUE CHARACTERISTIC of the chaplaincy is its ministry to all faiths and <u>even</u> to those of no faith. What continues to astound many is that this type of ministry can be effective and can be offered by a chaplain while he or she remains true to his or her own faith and faith group. This model of ministry can also teach the larger Church some important lessons about caring for people outside the church walls.

SCRIPTURAL FOUNDATIONS FOR CHAPLAINCY

NAVY CHAPLAINS LIKE TO TRACE their roots back to Genesis, Chapter One, *"The Spirit of God moved upon the face of the deep."* But Matthew, Chapter 25, verses 21 to 36, is most often cited by chaplains to justify their ministry beyond the parish. In this passage, Jesus says that when He comes He will say to those on the right,

> *Come, you who are blessed of my Father, take your inheritance, the kingdom prepared for you since the creation of the world. For I was hungry and you gave me something to eat. I was thirsty and you gave me something to drink. I was a stranger and you took me in. I needed clothes and you clothed me. I was sick and you looked after me. I was in prison and you came*

to visit me....whatever you did for the least of these brothers of mine you did for me." NIV

Go to Them

IN THE EXAMPLES WHICH JESUS cited, the needy probably would not have gone to the church for help. Therefore, the caregivers needed to go to them. The essence of the chaplain's ministry reflects the incarnational nature of Christ's work which is to go in person to the places where human need is the greatest.

Keeping Watch

SECONDLY, THE CHAPLAIN SEEKS TO recognize and meet the basic needs of people even before they address spiritual needs. Is this not also what Jesus urges when he speaks of giving food, clothes, shelter, water, and visitation to those who are or feel forgotten? Naomi Paget and Janet McCormack have an excellent exposition of Matthew 26:36-45 in their book The Work of a Chaplain, (pages 9 and 10). Jesus, on His way to the cross, asks the disciples, *"Could you men not watch with me one hour?"*(NIV) Keeping watch involves an active emotional and spiritual presence in addition to physical presence, according to Paget and McCormack. Often the chaplain is called to do no more than watch with people in their hour of crisis, sickness or death. This kind of ministry, Jesus said, was not to be neglected, as the disciples were tempted to do.

Certainly Jesus' story of the Good Shepherd going out to seek, find, and rescue the lost sheep recorded in Luke 15:4-7, is a powerful picture of chaplain ministry. Jesus' example of going outside the temple and synagogue, engaging people where they lived and worked, speaks of His strong endorsement of the need for this kind of ministry. In addition, the Bible repeatedly calls for His representatives to respect, love, and care for all people since all bear the image of God. After the great flood God says to Noah, *"I will demand an accounting...from every man...for the life of his fellow man."* (Genesis 9:5). We normally interpret this passage as referring only to the taking of a human life, but could it not also refer to our neglect of human life when we might have helped? This was the spirit of St. Martin who shared his cloak with the poor beggar and, in the spirit of Jesus, inspired others to follow his example. This is only a small portion of the many Biblical examples that still motivate men and women to answer the call to become chaplains. The chaplain model of ministry is finding wide and growing acceptance in and outside the Church today. As John Wesley rightly said of his ministry, "The World is my parish."

CHAPTER TWO
THE CHAPLAIN AS A PERSON AND A REPRESENTATIVE OF THE CHURCH

My assignment was to relieve a squadron chaplain, a Roman Catholic Priest, who had been serving a group of Navy ships deployed in the Far East. Upon reaching the appointed ship, I discovered that the chaplain had already departed several days earlier without leaving a note. Over months, I slowly pieced together his story. Apparently the chaplain had failed to adjust to Navy life. The unpredictable schedule of the ships, the challenging living conditions, and the Vietnam War had taken their toll on his morale. He had also failed to relate well to the ship's crew and found it more and more difficult to support the war in which we were engaged. So, he deserted his parish and post and caught a flight for home.

From all I could gather, the chaplain had been a successful priest in his Catholic parish where things were familiar, predictable, and relatively peaceful. But in this constantly changing environment at sea, he was frustrated and his frustration turned to anger and depression. He resented his assignment and he looked down on those he was sent to serve. His flock in return seemed to have rejected him.

On the other hand, some clergy excel in these kinds of challenges, preferring them to the daily predictable routines. What makes the difference? Does the chaplaincy require a certain kind of person or personality? I think so. We must be careful to acknowledge that all the gifts that are essential in a parish pastor are also essential in a chaplain. Not one should be missing. However, to these basic pastoral gifts must be added some special gifts for the chaplain. Let's discuss some of those special gifts as we consider the chaplain as a person.

The Chaplain's Added Gift Mix

FIRST, THERE IS THE GIFT of <u>ability to work with a secular staff</u>. Members of a secular staff do not always appreciate or understand the value of the chaplain's contribution to the team or to the institution. This conflict can make the chaplain's work more difficult. One chaplain found himself working with a secular staff that not only lacked religious faith <u>themselves</u> but took great delight in ridiculing the chaplain and the faith of his flock. Such staff members are in the minority, but they do exist and can become a source of profound testing for the chaplain. A good chaplain anticipates such opposition and works to defuse it. If that is not possible, the chaplain accepts it and keeps focused on the ministry at hand. Like Jesus who set his face toward Jerusalem, the chaplain sets his face representing Christ within the secular, as well as religious, institutions.

A second special gift the chaplain should possess is <u>the ability to minister to people of all faiths as well as to people of no faith.</u> This does not mean that the chaplain must deny his/ her own beliefs or faith group, but rather he/she must reach out to all people in order to help them connect with God. It also means the chaplain must not only know his/her own faith group and teachings, but he/she must also be familiar with the practices and teachings of other faith groups in order to help them freely practice their own religious faith as provided for under the Constitution.

<u>Ecumenical team work</u> is also a gift. Most clergy live their professional lives working, fellowshipping, training, and associating with clergy like themselves. Often they have gone to the same seminary or college. But most Free Methodist chaplains will find themselves working as a team member with a Roman Catholic priest, a Baptist, a Lutheran and even a Latter Day Saint or a Christian Science practitioner. Again, the chaplain will not be required to compromise his/her own religious convictions but must recognize that most communities in which they serve are diverse in their religious practices and this diversity must be respected.

The chaplain must also display the gift of <u>flexibility.</u> The parish pastor has some surprises in his or her daily duties but not to the degree as does a chaplain. The nature of the ministry settings makes them open to a high degree of crisis ministry. Crisis intervention is often the rule of the day rather than the exception. Chaplains minister to people whose lives have been disrupted with bad news, health and emotional issues, broken relationships, crime, fire loss, auto accidents and the violence and trauma of war. Every crisis demands flexibility on the part of the chaplain. Daily schedules often go out the window in order to meet these pressing needs. This is common ministry for the chaplain. In addition, the military chaplain must be ready to move out and around the world at a moment's notice. Sometimes they must leave spouse and children behind for extended and repeated periods of time. Those who lack the gift of flexibility need not apply.

Disciplined self-care is a vital gift. Dr. Tony Headley, Professor and Head of the Pastoral Care Department at Asbury Theological Seminary, has done extensive studies and writing on clergy self care. But what are considered major problems in general are often multiplied many times over in the lives of chaplains because of the added stress inherit in their ministry settings. This does not mean burnout is necessarily a greater threat to chaplains, but it does mean that they must know their limitations and have a positive plan to care for themselves. Otherwise, they will be unable to stay the course.

Finally, the chaplain must be ready to exercise a high degree of accountability. Most churches are very lax in requiring accountability from their pastors. On the other hand, the institutional settings require the same strict accountability from the chaplain they do from their other employees. This means that the chaplain must be on time to work and staff meetings, and must keep the supervisor informed of his/her whereabouts. The chaplain is also subject to work reviews, evaluations, audits, and numerous reports. Accountability includes obeying the rules and policies of the work place and supporting the mission of the institution. A failure to be accountable can be considered grounds for discipline or dismissal. Again, few clergy are held to this level of accountability.

The Chaplain as a Representative of the Church

THE CHAPLAIN IS FIRST A representative of the church or faith group that ordained and endorsed him/her. Secular institutions do not ordain their chaplains or act as a watch dog over the chaplain's religious teaching and practice. This is the task of the sponsoring Church or faith group. Some pastors have wrongly believed that clergy who join the chaplaincy leave their ordination vows behind. I have met some chaplains who erroneously thought the same thing. Wrong!

Sad to say, some have taken advantage of their geographical distance from the Church to also distance themselves emotionally and theologically from their denominations. Ultimately this is destructive to the chaplain's relationship to the endorsing Church and to the institutional setting which he/she serves. In fact, most institutional settings strongly encourage and support the chaplain's relationship with his/her faith group and will often provide the chaplain time and funds to keep this important connection.

In our denomination, the Church urges its chaplains to attend their Annual and General Conferences and keep connected with a local church where possible. Annual reports are required of every chaplain, both to their Conference and to their Endorsing Agent. Chaplains are also urged to participate in the Free Methodist Chaplains Association which exists for the mutual support of our chaplains and their families. The chaplains are also asked to make a regular monetary contribution to the Endorsing Office to assist the Director. So, the Church, the Endorsing Office, the Chaplains Association, and the chaplains' institutional settings all strongly support and encourage the chaplains to maintain ties to their endorsing body. The chaplain's ministry must always be seen by the chaplain and institution as an extension of the Church's ministry.

CHAPTER THREE
THE DEVELOPMENT OF THE FREE METHODIST CHAPLAINCY

THE ROOTS OF THE FREE Methodist chaplaincy can be traced back to World War II and the nation's urgent call for chaplains to minister to our troops. Prior to this time, records do not indicate the Church had a formal program or process to recruit, screen, and endorse clergy who felt called to be chaplains. The pressing needs of the war effort demanded the resources and support of the Church. When the Church saw its young men and women marching off to war, it was concerned for their spiritual welfare. It was mainly a question of how the Church could be with their own servicemen and servicewomen in their hour of greatest need and peril. The nation urged the churches to participate by sending their finest clergy to serve in uniform as chaplains.

Bishop Marston

OUR CHURCH RESPONDED ENTHUSIASTICALLY UNDER the able and energetic leadership of Bishop Leslie Marston. In fact, Bishop Marston deserves the title of the "Father of the Free Methodist Chaplaincy." He was elected Bishop in 1935. When World War II began, he was given responsibility for our chaplains. Almost single handedly he set up the endorsing process for our chaplains, kept the records, communicated with applicants and endorsed chaplains. Because we were one of the smaller denominations, he wisely contacted the larger Methodist Church and asked their endorsing bishop if they could assist our Church by acting as our final Endorsing Agent for chaplains. They agreed and an official endorsing procedure between the two Churches was put in place.

First, the Free Methodist chaplain candidate would apply for the chaplaincy through the Free Methodist Church. If the candidate received our Bishops' endorsement, they were then sent on for a final screening and endorsement by the Methodist Commission on Chaplains. If they approved the candidate, the chaplain then enjoyed a dual endorsement. However, if the Methodist Church refused endorsement, the Free Methodist church agreed to accept their decision as final and the candidate was sent home. It was an excellent relationship that lasted for nearly fifty years and served the church well. The Methodists treated our chaplains as their own. The initial administrative cost for this service levied by the Methodists was $6.50 per chaplain per year. By serving under the Methodist chaplain quota, the Free Methodist Church was able to greatly exceed their own small quota which would have been no more than six to eight chaplains total. We sometimes had as many as 22 chaplains or more serving on active duty at one time. We owe the Methodist Church a great debt of gratitude for their generous assistance to us during those years.

Health care, correctional, and Civil Air Patrol chaplains followed close behind our growing military ministry. In time, Bishop Marston shared his oversight of chaplains with Ernest Keasling who was the Servicemen's Director, a position we will describe later. However, Marston continued to keep his hand in the program well into the 1960s.

Period of Discouragement

FOR A SHORT PERIOD FOLLOWING WWII, strong voices from influential Church leaders discouraged the denomination from sending chaplains into the military because (1) pastors were needed in the local church and (2) because it was reasoned chaplains were not needed in the military when the nation was at peace. As a result, some clergy were thwarted from pursuing the call, while others who had applied were denied endorsement. In a few cases, this resulted in some fine candidates leaving our Church for other denominations that were more open to the chaplaincy. This was an unfortunate and painful period in our chaplaincy history. Although little documentation is available, it can be assumed that this peace-time attitude toward the military chaplaincy set the Free Methodist effort back a few years. A new Endorsing Agent would soon take the helm and would mark the end of this unfortunate period.

Chaplaincy: Being God's Presence in Closed Communities

Bishop Leslie Marston, Chairman
Chaplains Committee

Rev. Ernest Keasling,
Director of Servicemen

Chaplain Leon Hawley,
First Chaplain

Chaplain G. H. Gifford,
Second Chaplain

* All the pictures above were taken from the Free Methodist Magazine

Robert Crandall

RECORDS SHOW THAT IN 1962, Robert Crandall was given oversight of the Free Methodist chaplains and began to officially visit the chaplains in their settings as Endorsing Agent. For the first time, Crandall saw to it that funds were provided for chaplains to visit General Conferences. His efforts greatly advanced the morale of the chaplains by increasing the recognition of their ministry before the Church.

Lawrence Schoenhals

DR. LAWRENCE SCHOENHALS FOLLOWED CRANDALL as Endorsing Agent for Chaplains. His primary position was as Director of Higher Education and The Ministry for the denomination with Endorsing Agent as a secondary duty. Schoenhals was a very compassionate man and his reports show he was deeply moved by his visits with chaplains and their spouses. His reports also show that he had a deep understanding of the chaplains' stress and feeling of isolation from the Church. He made a passionate plea for Church leaders to visit chaplains and to send them notes and birthday cards. However, there is no evidence that such a response ever developed.

Bruce Kline

DR. BRUCE KLINE FOLLOWED SCHOENHALS in the position of Higher Education and the Ministry, and also assumed the Endorsing duties. Bruce and Kay Kline were a rare team. Chaplain spouses, for the first time, had a strong advocate in Kay. She looked to their needs and provided emotional support. In addition, Kay initiated, typed and produced the first official chaplain newsletter. Dr. Kline established the Chaplain Medallion Award, a beautiful medal presented by the Board of Christian Education and the Chaplains Endorsing Office to chaplains who had distinguished themselves as representatives of the Church to their ministry setting. Myron Henry, a Navy and Correctional Chaplain, was the force and mind behind the design of the medallion. Don Zimmerman, USAF also worked with Myron on the design during one of their meetings in Okinawa where Zimmerman was stationed. The kind and compassionate spirits of Kay and Bruce Kline again moved the Church's chaplaincy forward and made us stronger.

Dean Cook

UPON KLINE'S RETIREMENT, DEAN COOK was appointed Endorsing Agent. His appointment is noteworthy because he was the first chaplain to hold that position, a tradition that still continues today. The Board of Bishops had been responsive to a strong recommendation by the Chaplains Association that a chaplain be appointed to that position. Like other Endorsers, Cook, a former Navy chaplain, had another primary job as teacher and chaplain at Roberts Wesleyan College. During his tenure as Endorsing Agent, he devoted his summers and school vacations to visiting chaplains. In the beginning, he and Bishop Gerald Bates, who was assigned oversight of the chaplains, shared secretarial support and an office near the campus in North Chili, New York. Later, the Endorsing Office was moved into Cook's home and his wife, Ruth, then became his secretary. Cook wrote and published a chaplains' manual which was provided to military chaplain applicants. His doctoral thesis had dealt with the transition of Free Methodist clergy into the military chaplaincy and the manual was a part of his thesis. The study revealed a very high degree of job satisfaction among our military chaplains.

When President Clinton was elected to office, it appeared that there was a plan to introduce homosexual clergy into the military chaplaincy as a social experiment. At that time, several denominations threatened to withdraw their chaplains if they were forced to participate in this experiment. The Free Methodist Church and its chaplains were rightly concerned. As a result, Chaplain Cook wrote the Church's official position on the subject which was approved by the Board of Bishops and presented to the Chiefs of Chaplains. This stand by the Free Methodist Church and other denominations was no doubt instrumental in the Administration's changing its mind about using the military services as a social experiment.

In 1994, Cook was appointed to the Wilmore Free Methodist Church in Kentucky and the John Wesley Seminary Foundation at Asbury Theological Seminary. With the added responsibilities of the church and Foundation he made preparation to resign as Endorser Agent. However, before doing so, he recommended to the Board of Bishops that consideration be given to the Church assuming the sole role of Endorsing Agent for all our chaplains and no longer relying on the United Methodists to act as our final Endorsing Office. The reason given was that our Church was now large enough to provide the level of leadership needed to support our chaplains. After his resignation, Chaplain Harry Ansted, Colonel, Air Force Retired, was appointed.

Harry Ansted

ANSTED WOULD LEAD THE CHURCH in making this very important transition, disconnecting from the United Methodist Church and becoming our own Endorsing Office. This transition marked the end of a rich fifty-year relationship with the Methodist Commission on Chaplains. Chaplain Ansted, or "Bud" as he is affectionately called, would run the Endorsing Office out of his home near Riverside, California. With no secondary job to distract him, Bud would take this part-time position and make it nearly a full-time ministry. Because of his and his wife, Lois, generous gift of time and energy they were able to reach a number of watermarks that greatly advanced the Church chaplaincy.

Bud was respectful but fearless in presenting the needs and ministry of the chaplains before our Bishops, Board of Administration, and General Conference. Things were never dull when he was present. He and Lois traveled tirelessly and extensively, stateside and overseas, visiting and counseling chaplains. They made significant strides in expanding and improving the chaplains newsletter and greatly increased communications with chaplains. They brought chaplains together through professional conferences held in interesting settings with attractive and challenging speakers. Bud accomplished all of this, even though the Church's leadership had wondered aloud if, at his age, he was up to this level of energetic leadership! They totally underestimated Harry "Bud" Ansted.

Robert Barnard

IN 1999, BUD CHOSE TO retire again and Chaplain Robert Barnard, a retired Army Chaplain who had transferred into the Free Methodist Church from the United Methodists was appointed as his replacement. Bob was living in Wilmore, Kentucky, at the time and was working on his Doctoral degree in Management from the University in Oxford, England. For the next seven years, Bob capably led the chaplains, bringing the Endorsing Office fully into the Computer age. Though the former Endorsing Agents had used the computer in their work, Bob took it to a new level by developing a chaplain website, putting the budget and office records on computer and using e-mail to keep in touch with chaplains.

Also, a number of policies were proposed by Bob and adopted by the Board of Bishops which greatly strengthened the professional position of our chaplains and their relationship to their annual conferences. Evie, Bob's wife, accompanied him on many visits to chaplains and was warmly supportive of the spouses.

During Bob's tenure, Chaplain Howard Lehman, a chaplain at Deaconess Hospital in Oklahoma City, designed and handcrafted a beautiful wooden communion set which he presented the Chaplains Association and the Endorsing Office to be used by the chaplains when they came together for conferences and business meetings. The set is a remarkable work of art and a wonderful gift.

Rex Carpenter

IN 2007, REX CARPENTER, A recently retired Air Force Chaplain, was appointed Endorsing Agent. He remains in the position at this writing and has done much to update the office and set the course for the future. He and his wife, Louise, work out of their home in Hampton, Virginia, not far from Langley Air Force Base First Fighter Wing from which he retired in 2006. They spend a major amount of time visiting chaplains in their settings. He has also developed close working relationships with Bishop Matt Thomas, who has oversight of all chaplains, and with the Chaplains Association. In addition, he initiated a newly-designed newsletter that has wide distribution, not only amongst the chaplains but also among Church leaders and the national Church.

Chaplains Association

THIS HISTORY OF THE FREE Methodist chaplaincy would not be complete without a discussion of the significance of the Chaplains Association. By the late 1960s, concerned chaplains such as Randy Tucker, Myron Henry , Bud Ansted, Dan Hummer and Dean Cook were voicing the need for some kind of formal organization among the Church's chaplains for the purpose of mutual support and as a means of communicating their concerns to the general Church.

Work was begun on a constitution for a chaplains association, with Chaplain Randy Tucker assigned to write the document. Upon completion of the constitution, the chaplains met in 1988 at Spring Arbor College, along with Bishop Gerald Bates and Endorsing Agent Bruce Kline, and adopted it. For the first time, the Free Methodist Chaplains would now appear in the Church Yearbook as a recognized body and an official denominational ministry. This was a major achievement that would have important implications for the future growth and development of the Church's chaplaincy.

Preamble

The Preamble read as follows:

We, ordained Elders in the Free Methodist Church, serving under special Conference appointment as chaplains, do hereby organize to form an association in keeping with the constraints of the BOOK OF DISCIPLINE, Free Methodist Church of North America, for the purpose of sharing a common ministry, for discussing matters of common concern and formulating any policies that will significantly contribute to the life and ministry of chaplains endorsed by the Church; and for the spiritual and social enrichment of chaplains, spouses and families. It is in view of the integrity of the close bond of fellowship realized by pastor with fellow pastors, pastor with annual conference and pastor with congregation, that this association is formed, to promote a closer bond with fellow chaplains. The Chaplains Association intends to uphold, maintain and support the Free Methodist Church, its appropriate internal agencies, and the causes endorsed by the Church.

Purpose

UNDER ARTICLE II, IT STATES that the Association leaders may serve as an advisory and consulting body to the Endorsing Agent and the Board of Bishops. As the Association has grown so has this aspect of their role. The Association elected as their first President, Randy Tucker, honoring him for his hard work in bringing the Association to reality. The organization remains strong today, providing monetary support to the Office of the Chaplain Director, spearheading professional conferences, offering an opportunity for connection with other chaplains, and acting as a consultant to the Director and Board of Bishops.

Scholarship Fund

THE ASSOCIATION ESTABLISHED A SCHOLARSHIP fund to assist chaplains and chaplain candidates who wished to enroll in CPE training. Chaplain Tucker provided the initial funds to make the scholarship a reality and it remains active to this day.

Chaplain Bakwa Salumu Nendjo

IN THE 1980S THE ASSOCIATION voted to purchase a motorcycle for an African Free Methodist Army chaplain, Captain Bakwa Salumu Nendjo, who was serving in the Zaire Armed Forces. Chaplain Nendjo served in the 41st Commando Shock Brigade of the 411th Commando Battalion. He was known by Chaplain Ansted who had served as a volunteer missionary in Africa. When Ansted presented Bakwa's need to the Chaplains Association, the chaplains eagerly and generously gave several thousand dollars to buy him a motorcycle for use in visiting his troops at a distance. In addition, the chaplains raised funds to bring him to the General Conference in Seattle in 1989, where he met with the Chaplains Association. Chaplain Bakwa later sent a letter to the Association regarding the gift of the motorcycle which read as follows:

> May it be permitted me to present to you in this form, my strongest thanks for such praiseworthy act which you deigned to do for me for the better carrying out of my evangelistic and pastoral ministry to the Zairian Armed Forces. It was like a dream when I considered the project of buying me a means of travel….The motorcycle is here now and serves me well…I was like Timothy and my colleagues were to me as Paul. This motorcycle is dedicated to the ministry of bearing the gospel to souls lost and in despair. I invite you to assist me in prayer in order that I may be, day by day, a good and durable soldier, a persevering athlete, and a faithful worker…all in the service of the Lord."
>
> My greetings and gratitude in Jesus Christ
> Protestant Military Chaplain
> Rev. Bakwa Salumu Nendjo
> Captain

CHAPTER FOUR
MILITARY CHAPLAINCY

OUR STORY BEGINS WITH THE call of our country to come minister to the military's closed community as it entered World War II. Large numbers of chaplains were needed quickly. Our Church, along with many others, responded enthusiastically. Bishop Marston, as has been noted, stepped forward to lead this new challenge. Clergy who volunteered and were found to be qualified were given commissions as officers and were told to minister according to the authority of the church that endorsed them. The military made it clear that they did not establish a military religion, but rather received their ministry from the churches. This maintained the separation of church and state but placed the chaplains under a kind of dual responsibility. They were responsible to both the military and to their own endorsing body. However, in the case of the chaplains' religious practice, the church would be the final authority.

As early as 1775, the Continental Congress had authorized the presence and pay for chaplains. Title 10 of the U.S. Code formally established the Armed Forces Chaplaincy and defined its legal parameters. This Code has been challenged many times over the years by those who oppose the chaplaincy, but each time their efforts have failed to deprive our servicemen and women of their constitutional right to worship. The military chaplain assists members of the Armed Forces in claiming their right to the free expression of their religious faith in war and peace.

First Free Methodist Chaplains

PRIOR TO AMERICA'S ENTRY INTO WWII, we had only two military chaplains, both in the Army. Leon Hawley, graduate of Seattle Pacific College and member of the Columbia River Conference, joined the Army Reserves in 1934. About that same time he was assigned as Assistant District Chaplain with the Civilian Conservation Corps for the western United States. Hawley traveled from state to state visiting and ministering to CCC camps. In January 1941, prior to the attack on Pearl Harbor, Hawley was called to active duty by the Army Chaplain Corps. This, according to Church records, makes him our first chaplain.

Our second chaplain, C. H. Gifford, was a graduate of Syracuse University and Garrett Theological Seminary and a member of the Kentucky-Tennessee Conference. Gifford was commissioned into the Army Chaplain Corps in July of 1941 and saw duty on ships in three theaters transporting Army troops to war. Records show that his military career was cut short when he and the Army had differences over matters of conscience in the exercise of his duties. This was the first case in which our Church and the military worked together to resolve a chaplain's issue of conscience.

As mentioned earlier, Bishop Marston, working with the Methodist Bishop responsible for their Commission on Chaplains, came to an agreement whereby the Methodists would act as our Endorsing Agent for the military. This came about with the approval of the military services. According to the Methodist Commission record, this is how it unfolded. The parameters were as follows:

> Appointment to the chaplaincy of the Army and Navy were based on denominational quotas. These were in turn determined by the National Religious Census. Denominations whose numerical strength was limited, did not receive an appointment quota. Such was the case with the Free Methodists, Wesleyans, and Primitive Methodists.

Thus began a close and fruitful relationship with the Methodist Church that continued for over half a century. This relationship was recognized and celebrated in 1995 when the Free Methodist Church assumed the duties of establishing and providing for our own Endorsing Agent Office for military chaplains. The Methodist Church was more than generous during those early years and did much to process, train, visit and care for our chaplains. We owe them a great debt of gratitude.

With the help of the early Methodist Commission on Chaplains, the Free Methodists soon had many more chaplains on active duty than their normal quota would have permitted. Methodist Commission records found in Bishop Marston's files, show the following Free Methodist chaplains as being endorsed by the Methodist Church and serving in WWII:

Charles Ackley, Navy; William Allayaud, Army; Albert Darling, Army; Francis Fero, Army; Kenneth Fristoe, Army; Clayton Gifford, Army; Alvah

Harford, Army; Leon Hawley, Army; Robert Hayes, Army; Charles Kingsley, Army; Robert Klein, Army; Walter Mack, Army; Kendall Mayhew, Army; Owen Mullett, Army; Horatio Ogden, Army; Oliver Porter, Army; Merlin Probst, Army; John Robb, Navy; Forest Walls, Army; Robert Warren, Army; Harry Webb, Army; and George Whiteman, Army. This list may be incomplete but it reflects their best records at the time.

In 1945, President H.J. Long of Greenville College wrote an article for the college publication acknowledging the exceptional contribution of the military alumni chaplains. The article was accompanied by pictures of twenty chaplains who were graduates of the college. This was an extraordinary contribution for a small Midwest, Free Methodist college. They are to be congratulated for this exceptional contribution to our nation and church.

Columbia River Conference, for its size, made its mark on the chaplaincy also. Chaplains Hayes, Hawley, Ogden, and Darling all came from this one small conference and each distinguished himself by exceptional and faithful service, as we will see later.

In the mid-1940s, Bishop Marston wrote a series of articles for the Light and Life magazine entitled, "Religion and War". In these articles he addressed the freedom our chaplains enjoyed in conducting worship, preaching and ministering among the soldiers, sailors, Marines and airmen. Marston wrote, "Many chaplains felt more freedom in their preaching in the service than they did in their civilian pulpit." However at least one chaplain was transferred to a new command because he felt it would violate his conscience to perform certain assigned duties that he did not consider of a religious nature. Apparently some of those duties fell under the general category of "welfare of the troops." Though from a very conservative denomination and schools, they demonstrated an unusual degree of flexibility and common sense in the performance of their duties. Not only did these fine men represent Christ and the Church well under the toughest of conditions, but many excelled above the call of duty. They were awarded some of our nation's highest decorations and citations for their ministry.

Chaplain Leon Hawley and General Douglas MacArthur

WHEN PRESIDENT ROOSEVELT ORDERED GENERAL McArthur and his staff to escape from Corregidor in the Philippines, he and his wife fled to Australia. There, Chaplain Hawley ministered to the General's soldiers and Mrs. MacArthur. According to Hawley, Mrs. MacArthur attended chapel faithfully but the General was often away on behalf of his Pacific command. Later, when our troops landed in the Philippines and liberated the islands, Chaplain Hawley accompanied them and later began a G.I. Gospel Hour on a Manila radio station. This program later became the Far East Gospel Crusade Broadcast. Following the war, Chaplain Hawley would assist the Free Methodist Church in establishing our mission work in the islands.

Chaplain Charles Ackley

CHAPLAIN ACKLEY, ONE OF OUR few WWII Navy chaplains, wrote from the South Pacific in 1943, "This is our war and our future for which we struggle. I meet with nothing but growing respect for chaplains and a deep, sincere intent for the things of God. Men of the sea have time to think and they know the power of nature and it convinces them of the omnipotence of God."

Chaplain Robert Warren

CHAPLAIN WARREN, THE SON OF Bishop Warren, wrote from a remote Pacific Island about the same time, "We are right in the heart of a coconut grove. We have flies, ants, bugs, lizards and all the insects of the tropics. It rains seven days a week and our tents have no floors but where sin abounds, grace did much more abound." Several of the troops erected a 12' x 12' tent for worship and prayer. They soon outgrew it and erected a second tent, 20' x 30'. Here, Chaplain Warren preached and held evangelistic meetings several nights a week. He reported that soldiers always responded to the invitation to accept Christ, and on two occasions, more than ten came forward. They enlarged their chapel once again, adding 15 feet to the rear. Warren wrote, "The crowds have continued to grow until now they have decided to push out the walls on both sides. We just go to those services expecting conversions and we are seldom disappointed."

Chaplains Fero, Harford and Probst

FROM THE OTHER SIDE OF the world Chaplain Fero wrote from England, "I had the exceptional privilege of hearing the Prime Minister [Winston Churchill] address the House of Commons." Fero never explained how he came to get such an honored seat. Chaplain Harford wrote about his experience preaching in a chapel on a large bomber base. "We shared the chapel with several other faith groups. In the space of a few hours the chapel furniture and fixtures would be rearranged so as to accommodate a different group. Yet, no group was bothered or disturbed by all this or the rituals of each other." Chaplain Probst wrote of a moving experience while serving in combat in France in 1945:

Last Sunday evening after church, a soldier came back with me to my room to borrow an Army- Navy hymnal. He sat in my room and told me what a mess he had made of his life and how God had spoken to his heart during worship.... as we talked from another part of the building came the strains of the first Christmas carols of the season...'Hark the herald angels sing, glory to the new-born King. Let every heart prepare him room, and heaven and nature sing.' Over in the corner is a German supply parachute. I'm going to make an altar cloth out of it. Lord haste the day when men shall beat their swords into plowshares and their spears into pruning hooks...and their parachutes into altar cloths..... my roommate, an Army Lt. Colonel, is sitting here reading my Bible. What a thrill to see him reading the Bible..... What a contrast to another young colonel we knew that under the stress of the war took his .45 and blew his brains out. May God have mercy on his soul. He was only 35 years old....'Change and decay in all around I see; O Thou that changest not, abide with me.'

Chaplain Kenneth Fristoe

TIME AND AGAIN OUR CHAPLAINS gave unselfishly of themselves in order that the souls under their care might be ministered to by the Church. In 1945, Chaplain Fristoe, a graduate of Los Angeles Pacific College and Greenville College, and former Conference Suprintentendent of the California Conference, was serving with the 31st Division Artillery in the battle for the Philippines. In the course of his duties, he demonstrated great courage and sacrifice which won him the praise of his men and Commanding Officer. As a result he was recommended for and received the Bronze Star with this citation:

> Chaplain(Captain) Fristoe is recognized for meritorious achievement in connection with military operations against the enemy in Bukednan Provence, Mindanao, Philippine Islands. In order to provide religious services and administration to his men in scattered areas, he exposed himself to a great deal of danger. Several times Chaplain Fristoe travelled through sniper-infested areas alone, knowing the danger. He also exposed himself repeatedly to artillery fire ...at night. Although he was briefed of these

dangers, his sense of loyalty and devotion to duty caused him to press on. He waded swollen streams, walked muddy roads and crossed swamps to bring ministry and encouragement to his men. On one occasion while conducting worship his position was taken under enemy artillery fire; however, the chaplain never cancelled worship if humanly possible.

In 1946, Fristoe flew to Shanghai, China, for duty with General George Marshall's staff. While there, he officiated at a Chinese wedding in which General Marshall gave the bride away. Fristoe also reported to the Church that while there he had the opportunity to minister to General Marshall and Madame Chiang Kai-shek.

Chaplain George Whiteman

IN 1945, THE AMERICAN TROOPS liberated a number of Nazi concentration camps in Germany. One of our Free Methodist chaplains was present at the liberation of Norshausen. Chaplain Whiteman writes of this traumatic experience:

> It is impossible to describe a concentration camp. It is a literal hell. We saw the oven where the bodies were burned. Here 20,000 prisoners were held....we saw a pit full of the ashes of thousands of human bodies. No mother, no child or baby could escape. The Nazis were the master race, but masters only in the use of evil force. We went through the hospital ward and saw what was left of humanity after Hitler had done his worst. We were told that none of them would live. We live in America and have been deprived of a few luxuries. We do not know total war… and may God grant that we never shall know.

As the war drew to a close, the chaplains became involved in helping servicemembers prepare to return home. Equally important was the task of helping the nation welcome them home. Chaplain Whiteman wrote a classic and thoughtful article in 1945 on the subject of coming home. The article appeared in the church magazine and was titled, "More of Him Is Coming Home."

> We shall not soon forget that memorable Sunday afternoon when the electrifying news interrupted the radio programs of the world to announce the rescue of Captain

> Eddie Rickenbacker and his crew. Secretary of War Henry L. Stemsom, in his first meeting with the press after the return of the rescued to the States, said, 'He has come back. I think more of him came back than went away.' What was said of Captain Rickenbacker can be said of the GI Joe who returns to you. He has come back. I think more of him came back than went away.

Whiteman goes on to enumerate the ways in which he believes the servicemembers have grown through their powerful involvement in the war effort:

1. This man has discovered another self. He will be more considerate. He will be more loving and tolerant of people. He will be very much a realist.
2. He wants no bands or blaring trumpets. These he feels belong to those who never came back.
3. His greatest battle is about the cessation of hostilities. He knows that peace is not the spontaneous result of an armistice.
4. His religion is simple and sincere. He has done a lot of thinking and praying. Deeds mean more than creeds. He is more interested in simplicity of worship than frills. He is more interested in churches that make Christians than those that make Methodists, or Baptists, or Lutherans.
5. He has overcome many petty ideas. To keep up with him you will need to do the same.
6. He went away a boy, he comes home a man. More of him is coming back than went away.

POST WWII

IF YOU WERE TO OPEN the Free Methodist Magazine dated July, 1946, you would see the photo of an Army chaplain with this heading: "ANSTED RECEIVES PRESTIGE AS SEOUL UNIVERSITY HEAD." The article goes on tto say:

> Word has been received of the manner in which Captain Harry B. Ansted, formerly serving in Korea as a chaplain in the Free Methodist Church, was elevated to prestige and position, second only to that of the Governor General

of the Island; for that is the standing of the President of Seoul University, and Ansted is serving as its President. It was about February tenth when Chaplain Ansted went to the University to secure a speaker for a Tuesday evening service. Not being able to find his man, the chaplain was leaving when an American officer appeared and offered his aid. On learning that Ansted had been in education for over twenty years, the Officer directed him to report to the Department of Education. He did and the Director asked him ten rapid-fire questions and then announced that there was a job awaiting him. By February Ansted was acting as Officer-In-Charge of the University and two weeks later he was installed as University President. Chaplain Ansted took his discharge from the US Army in Korea and continued on as University President while working with the G.I. Gospel House.

(The University was soon to grow to a student body of nearly15,000 students.) Chaplain Ansted never dreamed that his leadership of our small Wessington Springs College would prepare him for leadership of this great Korean University. Surely there is a fulfillment here of the biblical injunction that those who are faithful over little will be given responsibility over much.

THE CHURCH COUNCIL FOR MEN IN SERVICE

ALTHOUGH NOT DIRECTLY RELATED TO the chaplains' work, the Church's separate ministry to servicemen and servicewomen was highly commendable. The Church Council for Men in Service was created to support our Church members and Sunday School members away from home. The Council provided a link between the Church and the serviceperson by letters, and by providing free of charge such church publications as the Free Methodist Magazine, the Evangel, and other devotional literature. This flyer went out to all Free Methodist Churches in December of 1943:

> Seven thousand men from your homes are on the roster of the Council. The Council is the connecting link between our church and these men....many of these men are great soul winners. Many are real missionaries. They are messengers of the gospel. They hold prayer meeting and other services.

They practice personal evangelism. Shall we not as a Church do our utmost to support these men—to keep their morale at the highest possible level.

Every church was urged to give a dollar per member to support the cause. In addition, each church was to set aside a Servicemen's Sunday to promote this ministry to "our boys." Later the Council became the Servicemen's Department with its own director. Certainly no church for its size did more for their service people than did our small Church. It was estimated that the Free Methodist Church ministered to over 11,000 servicemen and servicewomen.

Fuchida Testimony

ALTHOUGH STRICTLY SPEAKING THE RELATIONSHIP between Sgt. Jacob DeShazer (Doolittle Raider on Japan) and Capt. Mitsuo Fuchida (leader of the attack on Pearl Harbor) is not a chaplain story, still it is one of the most fascinating and miraculous stories to come out of WWII. These two military men on opposite sides of the war, chanced to meet and God did a wonderful work in and through each of them. Both men became ordained ministers – DeShazer, a Free Methodist missionary and Fuchida, a Presbyterian pastor. Although DeShazer's testimony is recorded in several publications, Captain Fuchida's testimony is less known. Here are his words in an article entitled, "I Led the Air Raid on Pearl Harbor" published in the September 5, 1950 "Free Methodist" Magazine. He wrote this after being a Christian only one month:

> It was 3:19 a.m. according to Japan time, which was December 7, 7:49 a.m. Hawaii time. My heart was ablaze with joy with my success in getting the whole main force of the American Pacific Fleet in hand, and I put my whole effort into the war that followed it with strong hatred toward America, the results of which was that misery which is clear to everybody today.
>
> Aviators Hate America
>
> Why were we aviators filled with such strong hatred toward America then? Of course, we aviators then had neither hatred nor enmity toward American people as individuals, but the Board of Supreme War Command in Japan was strongly convinced that the destiny of the war was wholly

dependent upon the success or failure of the Pearl Harbor attack. Hence, in order to secure unfailing success in that strategy, the military high command accused America with such strong words as, 'brutal and proud America, the long-time enemy', only to create increased hatred of the aviators toward America. Having thus started participation in war, I devoted myself to conducting warfare through the following four years, presenting myself as a most patriotic and faithful soldier to the mother country.

Crashes into the Sea

During these four years, I faced death several times, including six crashes into the sea, but was miraculously saved every time to survive and see the war's termination. After the war and 25 years of Navy service, I retired and took myself to farming but it was indeed a path of thorns to me. I had never in my life realized so keenly the unreliability of other men during these years. I was strongly convinced that one's own ability was all he could rely upon, and consequently I worked diligently in silence, giving a cold glance to the world affairs around. The new career that I started from nothing, as it were, was so insignificant and slow, like an ant's progress. Nevertheless, as time passed on I built my house and digged the well, but my life during these years was no other than a reenactment of the story of Robinson Crusoe.

Begins to Think of God

Thus my lonely life dragged on. But in the meantime as I continued living in the closer relationship to the earth, [I was] feeling ashamed of my former godless idea that man's power and ability was his only trustworthy resource. I had never been an atheist. But I was brought up on circumstances of little religious atmosphere: consequently I grew up to manhood without any religion and later enlisted in the Navy. Therefore I held the former "War Catechism" as my only ideology.

With the termination of the war the national aspect was altogether transformed and Japan stepped out for the reconstruction of the nation with a slogan 'Peace'. Four years have elapsed since, and in these years I have been watching the constant change of social phenomena but with cold eyes. Nevertheless, I could not help but love the mother country with her mountains and rivers irrespective of good or bad. Accordingly, my mind has been constantly set on the problem as to what would be the proper way for Japan to exist hereafter. Finally, I arrived at the conclusion that the only way for the Japanese to survive and prosper would be to have every one of the Japanese people thoroughly made peaceful, irrespective of other nations' conditions.

"No More Pearl Harbor"

However, my militarily-specialized mind saw in the prevalent world conditions a possible danger of another war and another Pearl Harbor. Therefore, with the sincere desire to warn the people I determined to send out into the world a book entitled 'No More Pearl Harbor' no matter how insignificant my work might be. As my writing progressed, however, I came to realize in my appeal for 'No More Pearl Harbor' there must be an assurance of a transformation of hatredamong mankind to true brotherly love. So long as mankind remained in opposition to one another, within the frame of nationality, the only consequence would be the destruction of civilization. In the midst of these thoughts, one day in Tokyo at Shibuya Railroad Station at a Pocket Testament League' street meeting, I received a Christian pamphlet. The pamphlet was the testimony of Mr. Jacob DeShazer entitled 'I Was a War Prisoner of Japan.' At the first glance my mind was captivated and I read it through with great enthusiasm. One portion of the pamphlet interested me particularly, and that was the confession of Mr. DeShazer that during his imprisonment he had a strong desire to read the Bible. He recalled to mind that he had heard about Christianity which could transform human hatred to true brotherly love. This portion, as I read, drew my mind to the same state and with a desire to read the Bible. I purchased one and started reading. Before covering the first 30 pages, my mind was strongly impressed and captivated.

"This is It"

'This is it!' I was strongly convinced. I concluded that the true Realization of 'No more Pearl Harbor' was no other than to expect Christ's second coming and to endeavor to prepare men from all over the world worthy of welcoming Christ's return. As a first approach toward this, I was convinced that I should first of all become a good Christian. Thus, I contacted the Pocket Testament League representatives who showed me from the Bible how to become a Christian. I then opened my heart and accepted Jesus as my personal Savior on April 14, 1950. Today is just one month since I was saved. Naturally I am still inthe early stages of Christian growth, but I feel great joy in my daily Bible readings and my heart is filled with peace as I kneel to pray. Moreover, I think I can say today without hesitation that God's grace had been constantly set upon me and guided me even before I came to know Christ. God has revealed to me the way of salvation through the atoning blood of Jesus Christ. I decided to believe whatever is revealed in the Bible, accept it, and stand as His witness, telling others the truth with the help of the Lord.

On the front page of the book DeShazer by C. Hoyt Watson, is what may be the most profound photograph to come out of World War II. It is entitled "No longer enemies." In the picture Captain Fuchida and missionary DeShazer, sit on a couch in DeShazer's Japanese living room, reading the New Testament together.

KOREAN CONFLICT TO VIETNAM ERA

When WWII ended, several of our chaplains were released from active duty and returned to pastorates and other ministries. Only a few remained on active duty. Peace was short lived, however, when in 1951 North Korea invaded the South, touching off a major conflict. American troops, along with the United Nation Forces, were called upon to enter the conflict. General Douglas McArthur, was assigned Commander. World War II-hardened and trained troops who had been sent home were now called back to duty. This included a number of our Free Methodist chaplains. Chaplains such as Porter, Ackley, Mullet, and Ogden were ready to go.

These were joined by two new chaplains who had seen combat duty during WWII in non-chaplain roles. Roscoe Bell, a former Navy corpsman with the Marines, was now a pastor in Richland, Washington. Bell volunteered to return to service as an Air Force chaplain. His story will be told in more detail later. Erwin Beitelschies, who had served in WWII as a bombardier in a flight crew, was now ordained and commissioned as an Air Force chaplain. Beitelschies later changed his name to Ray. Lowell Ronne, a WWII Army Air Force officer, would also return as a chaplain. The Air Force ranks were enlarged again as Bud Ansted, son of Chaplain Harry Ansted, was endorsed and entered the service, along with. Clason Rohrer, and John Hoyt. The unusual interest in the Air Force can probably be traced to the separation of the Army Air Force from the Army in 1946 and the establishment of the Air Force as a separate branch of the Armed Services.

Chaplain Kenneth Fristoe

FOLLOWING GRADUATION FROM COMMAND AND Staff College, Kenneth Fristoe was assigned as Deputy Staff Chaplain for the Far East Command. In this capacity he assisted the Staff Chaplain with all chaplain assignments and supervision relating to Korea - a job with no small responsibility.

Chaplain Oliver Porter

OLIVER PORTER WAS TRANSFERRED FROM Heidelberg, Germany, to the 24th Infantry Division, fighting in Korea. His first assignment was to minister to new replacements arriving from the States. His soldiers were put through special training to prepare them for the front lines. Porter stated that the new troops, facing combat just days ahead, were highly receptive to the Gospel and he saw soldiers accept Christ nightly through his ministry. Later, Porter was assigned as Assistant Division Chaplain for the 24th Division.

Chaplain Horatio Ogden

WHEN AN AGREEMENT WAS REACHED between North and South Korea to exchange prisoners of war, the operation was dubbed "Operation Big Switch." Chaplain Ogden was one of five chaplains chosen to assist in the processing of our returned prisoners - a sensitive and delicate assignment. Ogden wrote of his experience in these words: "Daily caravans of ambulances wound their way across 'No Man's Land' bringing American and UN prisoners to Freedom Village. Here they shed their prisoners' uniforms and were greeted by our chaplains and offered Holy Communion at altars set up for this special purpose." These returning men often looked dazed as they tried to comprehend their transition from captivity and suffering to freedom. Ogden said the trees along the path that led to Freedom Village were filled with shoes and clothing the prisoners had tossed into the air in anticipation of their new life and new beginning.

It should be noted here that the Servicemen's Department Director, Ernest Keasling, visited Korea in 1953 to see Chaplain Ogden as he ministered at Freedom Village. During this visit he was able to observe American prisoners coming home

Chaplain Erwin Ray [Beitelschies]

BOMBARDIER-TURNED-CHAPLAIN, ERWIN RAY WAS SENT to the Fifth Air Force in Korea to minister to a number of small units dispersed throughout South Korea and, in one case, to a unit behind enemy lines. As our Free Methodist chaplains were all prone to do, he gave himself totally to the task. Upon observing the chaplain's zeal, his Commanding General nominated him for the prestigious Alexander D. Goode Award, (an award in honor of the four chaplains who had given their life vests to soldiers , and who went down with the USS DORCHESTER). Chaplain Beitelschies (Ray) was selected for the award and invited to New York City for the presentation by Major General Charles Carpenter, Chief of Air Force Chaplains. The citation read in part: "Chaplain Beitelschies showed exceptional steadfastness, courage, and clarity in his duties as well as a deep abiding spirit of selflessness and sacrifice."

Chaplain Harry "Bud" Ansted, Son of a Chaplain

OF ALL THE CHAPLAINS WHO have served the church, Harry (Bud) Ansted stands out as our greatest cheerleader and encourager. For over fifty years, Harry has been a chaplain or working to promote chaplains. Although now in their eighties, Harry and his wife, Lois, still organize our Chaplain Professional Conferences and act as gracious hosts. A plain spoken man, Harry has always been known for his enthusiasm, creativity, humor and spirituality. He confesses that he never intended to be a career Air Force Chaplain. He wanted to join the reserves. Chaplain Leon Hawley wrote a letter of recommendation for him to the recruiter. Bud applied and was accepted. The Air Force then asked him if he would come on active duty. Lois said she would follow him if he didn't go to Texas. His orders read, "Sheppard AFB, Wichita Falls, Texas." In his own words he describes what happened next:

> I was assigned to an area that had been a basic training area but just as I arrived they moved all the basic trainees out.

Chaplaincy: Being God's Presence in Closed Communities

> I was left with a chapel and no people. The Installation Chaplain assigned me a new chaplain support man who had just finished basic training. What the Installation Chaplain didn't know was that the man was a graduate of the University of Arizona and a member of the American Guild of Organists…and had directed the University Choir.

It just so happened that the Commanding Officer of the Base was looking for someone to lead a base choir for special ceremonies and events and to represent the base to the public. Harry volunteered for the mission using his new man as the choir director. The choir quickly grew.

> At first six showed up but one was a lyric tenor so we learned to sing in unison and went to several churches where we sang, 'God of our Fathers' in unison and then the tenor had several numbers. We were well received. After the choir grew to 30 we went all over doing concerts.

This was classic Bud. "Take what you have and make something good out of it for the Lord."

The following antidote describes how his own prejudice had limited his ministry to his flock:

> I had strong opinions about the use of alcohol. I had determined that I would not join the Base Club [usually a requirement for all Air Force officers] or go to cocktail parties. One time I went to a squadron party on the beach. A young airman came up to me to talk. He was quite inebriated. He said as we parted, 'Well at least our chaplain comes to our parties'. My whole focus changed and I realized that I needed to be where the troops were if I was going to minister to them….

Chaplains who fail to learn this basic truth usually do not last long in the service. The non-threatening atmosphere of a ship, squadron, and base or work-center party often becomes the opening for the troops to approach the chaplain and vice versa.

In this last story we see and hear the humor and plain speaking that is so much a part of Bud's personality:

> At Hill AFB in Utah…I had just been made Installation Chaplain. The Commanding General had been a SAC commander…[He] was very stern and everyone was afraid

of him. He never came to chapel. It was Thanksgiving time and he had a Commanders Call. He said to me so that all could hear, 'Chaplain, I received an invitation from the Salt Lake Cathedral but I did not receive an invitation [to the Thanksgiving service] from the Base Chaplain. I replied, 'General, all our regular parishioners know that we have a Thanksgiving Day Service but if you would like a special invitation I would be happy to send you one.' Everyone was shocked and wondered what the General would do.

The General just smiled but must have secretly admired the Chaplain for having taken him on. However, it could have been the end of Bud's promising career for embarrassing the General publically, even though he deserved it.

Chaplain Ansted speaks of Dr. Claude Watson visiting his base on behalf of the Church. Dr Watson, in his late eighties at the time, had just been awarded his private pilot's license. The General was impressed and they hit it off. For the next three hours they talked airplanes as they toured the base together. This visit points up the importance of official visits by Endorsing Agents to their chaplains' ministry settings. Commanding Officers need to know that churches support their chaplains and appreciate the mission of the military to keep America safe.

Chaplain Lowell Ronne

As mentioned earlier, Ronne had risen from the enlisted ranks to a commission in the Army Air Force in WWII while serving in a bomber squadron in Okinawa. After the war, he got out of the service, prepared for ordination, and was assigned a church. By 1954, he was feeling called back to the military as a chaplain. However, his call came during the "discouraging years" when Church leaders had felt it more important for seminary graduates to be assigned local churches than to enter the chaplaincy. Some even argued that the military chaplaincy was not needed in peace times and was a semi-religious kind of ministry. Ronne was dissuaded from applying. However, he did not give up and his application was finally approved. We can all be glad that Chaplain Ronne persisted for he went on to have a distinguished military chaplain career, rising to the rank of Colonel.

Chaplain Roscoe Bell

Chaplain Roscoe Bell, USAF, who was referred to previously, served during three wars: WWII, the Korean Conflict and Vietnam. Roscoe married Betty before he shipped out to the Pacific to serve as a Navy corpsman with the Third Marines in WWII. Bell served eighteen months of combat duty and took part in the invasion of Guam. Following Chaplains School in 1955, he and Betty received orders to England but the orders were cancelled when their four-year-old son Ronald was diagnosed with acute leukemia. Instead of England, they were sent to Hamilton Air Force Base in California to be near Letterman Army Hospital. In spite of all efforts, their beloved son died in a little over three and a half months.

In 1960 Roscoe was assigned to Clark Air Force Base in the Philippines, where Betty and their new daughter joined him. At Clark, Chaplain Bell led one of the largest Christian Education programs in the military service. Using 16 military buses for transportation, he built a Sunday School comprised of approximately <u>one thousand students</u>. During the Christmas season they collected and gave thousands of gifts to children in the Manila slums. In addition, they hosted a number of Free Methodist missionaries in their home who were coming and going from the field.

In early 1963, the Bells were sent to Malmstrom Air Force Base in Montana, where he was assigned to the Air Force's first Minute-Man Missile Wing. Among his many other duties was to visit the crews in the missile-silo complexes far out in the desolate desert. In 1966 it was off to Thailand where Roscoe ministered to our Air Force bases as well as to American servicemen and servicewomen billeted in hotels in Bangkok. One of his memorable experiences was leading a group of Airmen on a tour of the infamous River Qwai where a number of British and Dutch soldiers are buried. Their terrible suffering and yet courageous fight to survive the cruelty of the Japanese is recorded in the powerful movie, "Bridge Over the River Qwai."

Later Roscoe and his family were sent to Misawa, Japan. Here, Roscoe and Betty had the high privilege of hosting missionary (formerly Sergeant) Jake DeShazer and Captain Mitsuo Fuchida in their home. (See our earlier reference to these two men at the end of the World War II section.)

Their last assignment took the Bells to Edwards Air Force Base where the United States tests the newest military aircraft and where the space shuttle lands when weather is unfriendly in Florida. Here, upon his retirement, Chaplain Bell was awarded the Bronze Star medal to add to his eleven other awards. The Church recognized his leadership gifts and elected him to be the Superintendent of the Columbia River Conference, a position he held for nine years.

Chaplain John Hoyt

LEST WE FORGET THAT WHILE some are called to serve in conflicts, others minister in equally important places, helping serve those who keep the peace.

John Hoyt, his wife, Connie, and three children received orders to the other side of the world, Oslo, Norway. This NATO Headquarters needed a chaplain to minister to their staff and families. John was selected as the chaplain qualified to do so. Under his creative leadership there was built a strong and growing religious community. While in Norway he travelled monthly to Copenhagen, Denmark, to hold worship services for the American Embassy. In this unusual ministry, John had to be able to minister to all ranks and all branches of the services with grace, compassion, and respect for all his flock. His selfless spirit also added to the great tradition of the Free Methodist Chaplaincy.

As a note of interest, Chaplain Don Zimmerman, also an Air Force chaplain, served in this same assignment from 1985 to 1988. He attests to Chaplain Hoyt's skillful development of this fine ministry appointment, which not only included ministry to NATO personnel but also the recruitment, contracting, and supervision of civilian clergy to assist in this broad requirement. In 1988, Dr. Bruce Kline, then Chaplain Endorsing Agent, was guest speaker at the NATO Headquarters Prayer Breakfast at Oslo. Chaplain Don Zimmerman was Project Officer for this special annual event.

The Korean Conflict ended with an Armistice, not a peace treaty. This was also the beginning of the period we call the "Cold War." Communism was seen as a world threat. America would lead the cause to contain it, which meant that we would need a strong military, and with it, a strong Chaplains Corps for each major service.

VIETNAM

BY THE EARLY 1960S, AMERICA became embroiled deeper in the Vietnam conflict. The defeat of the French had left a vacuum in that area of the world and America's policy to contain Communism was being challenged. It seemed inevitable that our forces were going to be sucked into this Indo-China vacuum. As the American military began to build up its numbers, more slots opened for chaplains. Chaplains Tucker, Carroll, Henry, Timm, Bailey, Cook, Bouck, Buckley and Dollar all added their names to the Free Methodist roster of chaplains. Harvey Bailey would soon see fierce combat duty with his Army unit, and would be awarded the Silver Star for his exceptional ministry under fire. Chaplains Tucker and Timm would also find themselves in harm's way as they served in-country. Bouck, Carroll and Henry would see combat duty along the Vietnam coast aboard Navy Destroyers and other ships. Cook would see Vietnam from the sea and ashore as he served in support of Marines, Navy ships and Riverine Forces. His Vietnam experiences are recorded in his book

Salt of the Sea, published in 2005. Before this nine-year war would be over it is estimated that nearly 2,000 chaplains - Navy, Army and Air Force – would serve in the conflict. Never before had our troops, airmen and sailors receive such quality spiritual care. This was due to the lessons learned from the past, the high mobility of our chaplains, and the number of evangelicals who came in as chaplains. These evangelical chaplains filled the ranks left by the refusal of more-liberal clergy to participate because of their opposition to the war.

Vietnam also added a new dimension to the chaplains' duties. The military began to understand that to win the war we would have to win the hearts of the people. A plan was devised to engage in civic action projects. This meant going into the communities and villages to build or repair schools and churches. It also meant sending doctors and dentists out among the civilian villages to provide limited health care and counseling. Since the trust factor was a key element, the chaplains were the obvious ones to help lead these projects. As a result, many worthy and needy charitable works were done which resulted in much good will between the people and the military members. Often the Marines, soldiers, airmen and sailors gave generously of their own time and money for these projects.

Chaplain Myron Henry

IN 1966 AS THE WAR was heating up, Myron Henry, a Navy chaplain serving aboard a destroyer, wrote a piece for the Free Methodist Magazine entitled, "The Circuit Riding Chaplain" which reflected his own ministry at sea. Having been a circuit riding chaplain myself, this writer feels the article paints an excellent picture of the common experience of Navy chaplains:

> Hanging in a 'horse collar' beneath a helicopter, dangling over the deck of a carrier, the Padre of the Sea begins his visits to his congregations. Every Sunday, weather permitting, in an evolution dubbed 'Holy Helo', the Destroyer chaplain makes his rounds. The Sunday starts early, sometimes at sunrise. The chaplain dons his orange flight suit, helmet, life vest, worship kit, tape recorder, and with some survival gear in his pockets makes his way to the fantail(stern) of the ship to await the incoming chopper. The chopper arrives and the pilot flies the helicopter in circles above the ship as it steams on course. Finally when the ship is ready the pilot approaches and hovers his craft some 30 feet above the bobbing stern of the small ship. The helicopter lowers a small cable to which is attached a sling. The chaplain slips

himself into the sling and clinging to all his gear gives the helicopter a thumbs up, the signal to start hoisting. In a moment's time he is hoisted into the air and pulled safely inside the helicopter. Off they fly several miles to another small ship. Again they circle the ship and when all is ready they hover over the rising and falling deck. The crewman places the chaplain into the sling again and he is motioned to sit in the open door. The crewman now engages the cable, the chaplain slides out and is lowered to the ship below. He is then met by the Officer of the Deck and the ship's Lay Leader and escorted to the location of the worship service which has already been set up. Although all ships do not have a chaplain assigned, they are equipped with worship equipment and hymnals. After worship and greetings, the helo returns and the chaplain is caught up into the air and flies off to another ship.

Myron ends his description of the circuit riding chaplain by saying,"Everyone deserves to hear the good news...."

Chaplains Connecting in Hawaii Duty

IN THE EARLY 1970S SOMETHING happened that seldom occurs among Free Methodist military chaplains. Three Free Methodists received orders for simultaneous duty in Hawaii. Bud Ansted, now a Colonel, was sent to a Pacific Staff at Wheeler AFB in the center of Oahu. Randy Tucker was assigned to Fort Shafter Army Base with duty at Fort DeRussy on Waikiki Beach. Dean Cook was assigned to the Marines at Headquarters Marine Corps Pacific at Camp Smith which also hosted the Commander of the Pacific and his joint staff. Under Ansted's leadership, they got together regularly to the great delight of all chaplains and their families. Again, in the 1980s the unthinkable happened again. This time, four Free Methodist chaplains received orders to Hawaii, Cook, Timm, DeMond and Schwab. They, too, enjoyed regular times of fellowship which served to strengthen all involved.

LEAVING THE VIETNAM ERA AND LOOKING EAST

WITH THE ENDING OF THE Vietnam War, our nation needed a lot of healing as did the military. For the first time we had not won the war, although we had lost over 50,000 fine young Americans. But the nation's eyes would now begin to look toward the Middle East where tensions were rising between Israel and Lebanon, Jews, Christians, and Muslims. Few would have dreamed that over thirty years later this part of the world would still hold us hostage to its conflicts.

New names are now added to the Endorsing Agent's roster, names like David Ballew, Army; Ben Belcher, Navy; Ken Carpenter, Army; Robert Stanton, Army; Don Zimmerman, Air Force; David Thompson, Navy; Larry Racster, Army; Harold Hannum , Army; Dennis Demond, Army; Rex Carpenter, Air Force; Kirby Bertholf, Army; Jon Wright, Army; Herstel Carter, Navy; and Gary Tugan, Navy. Of these chaplains, one is chosen to demonstrate what could be called a textbook career which spanned thirty years. That chaplain is Kenneth Carpenter.

Chaplain Kenneth Carpenter

KENNETH CARPENTER WAS FROM HAMPTON, Virginia, a Navy town. While attending Trinity Seminary in Chicago, he met Dr. James Mannoia who was teaching a class there and Jim introduced him to the Free Methodist Church. Kenneth joined the church in 1970, pastored four years and felt called to the military chaplaincy. Even though he hailed from a Navy town, he wanted to join the Air Force, but since no openings were available, he joined the Army instead in 1974. Kenneth had no previous military experience and had no immediate family members in the service, so he had a lot to learn. After Basic School he received orders to Fort Sill, Oklahoma , home of the Army Field Artillery. Here, Carpenter would meet a Supervisory Chaplain who would take special interest in him, and would be his mentor for much of his career.

In his own words,"...He (Bernie Windmiller and his wife Esther) taught Jonna and me much about military ministry and culture...his mentorship then and later was an awesome blessing from God and instrumental in enabling me to develop and grow professionally." These words are full of truth. Elisha had his Elijah, Moses his Jethro, Joshua his Moses, David his Samuel, and the twelve disciples had their Jesus. The chaplain is blessed who finds a good mentor early in their career.

Drawing upon the wisdom and guidance of his mentor, Chaplain Carpenter rose steadily through the ranks, becoming one of the Army's most senior Colonels. He was assigned an astonishing variety of chaplain duties, which included Battalion Chaplain, Brigade Chaplain, Post Chaplain, Medical Center Chaplain, Community Chaplain, Area Chaplain, and for a short time, NATO Force Chaplain. His ministry included serving chapels, training commands, engineers, logistics commands, artillery commands, as well as management and staff positions. Much of his career was devoted to supervising chaplains and their support personnel along with major religious programs. During his thirty years he saw firsthand our nation's transition from the Cold War in Europe. Carpenter would witness the transition from hostile Russian troops and walls, to the opening up of roads into Russia and Eastern Europe, and finally the unification of Germany. He would also see the conflicts in Bosnia and the Middle East.

America's Bicentennial, 1976

IN 1976, OUR NATION CELEBRATED its bicentennial. At the time, this writer was deployed to the Mediterranean aboard the USS AMERICA, one of our attack carriers. Terrorism was on the increase and Lebanon was in conflict, becoming more unstable by the day. The AMERICA and her Task Force was ordered to the Eastern Mediterranean to prepare for possible evacuation of our Embassy and other Americans in Lebanon. The ships took up station off the coast and assisted in the rescue of the Embassy staff and other key people whose welfare could no longer be guaranteed by the Lebanonese Government. However, the most traumatic event was yet to happen a few hundred miles to the east in Iran.

The Shah of Iran had tied his government securely to the West, and particularly, to the United States. In doing so, he had purchased large amounts of American military equipment and invited American military advisors to help train his armed forces in their use. This had alienated the more conservatives Muslims who resented the American presence in the country and the intrusion of western culture upon their Islamic values. A powerful mullah, Khomeini, was in exile in France where he led the opposition against the Shah. Khomeini called for the expulsion of the American presence.

Chaplain Harry Timm

JUST AS EVENTS IN IRAN were becoming more unstable, Free Methodist Army Chaplain Harry Timm received orders to Iran to minister to the Americans stationed there. It was an accompanied tour which meant that he could take his wife, Mary Belle, and their twelve-year-old daughter, Shelly, and the family dog. The other two older children would remain in the States. Mary Belle and her daughter shared their experience with us, giving us insight into what military families experience in uncertain times. Mary Belle writes:

> We left in August and I remember flying into Tehran and seeing how brown and dry everything looked. We stayed in a hotel waiting to find a place to live. Harry's chaplain's

assistant kept our dog while we looked for an apartment. One morning he came to work and held up the leash saying the dog had broken loose and he was unable to find her. After many days of looking we gave up. What a heartbreak, for she was part of the family.

Shelly recalls this painful incident from the point of view of a young girl without friends, alone in a strange land:

> We had our beloved dachshund, Buffy, with us. Because we were unable to keep her in the hotel, Dad asked his assistant to watch her. When he announced that the dog was lost, with hope and fear we searched the streets, asking people who didn't speak English if they had seen her. We walked the "jube" ditches, large cement ditches full of rocks and debris found all around Tehran, calling for her and searching. My dog was gone, in a foreign place. We prayed that she might have met a quick death, or been taken by kind people. To this day I can be right back there walking the ditches with hope and fear and I still cry over Buffy - she was my best friend.

When the administrators were preparing Chaplain Timm's orders, they asked him, "What color is your daughter's hair?" When he had answered "blond", they replied that the Iranians considered light hair special, something to be revered. Chaplain Timm shared this with his family but they did not understand its impact on a little girl of twelve years. Shelly went on to say,

> I had not paid much attention to what he had said about that [the hair]. The truth of it was realized when we went out in the car. Men stared and smiled all the time, some even put their hands through the open car window and touched my hair. It scared me. I quickly took to laying down in the back seat when we went anywhere. Iran was hot and dusty, with muted colors and a mixture of poverty and wealth, old and new. I remember seeing roadside signs in Farsi and seeing the pictures of the Shah. I saw women covered from head to toe and women in blue jeans and high heels. Traffic was chaos and no rules seemed to exist. Americans were considered upper class. I waited outside our gated house for transportation to the Tehran American School. The van-

type school bus had two Iranian drivers and was equipped with bullet proof windows and curtains.

Shelly went on to say that her school life with other American children was pretty normal. Mary Belle found life in Tehran a bit dreary. She mainly stayed at home while Shelly was at school and Harry was at work. Often, chaplains live on a military base and the wives will be among other wives with whom she feels close and can socialize. In Tehran, Mary Belle was in a second-story apartment above the Iranian property owners. They were friendly but knew limited English. Chaplains quickly find their niche at work, but wives can find themselves isolated and alone when moving to a new place of duty. Being alone during the day in a strange country with a strange language and growing political tensions would certainly be enough to place the chaplain's family under great stress. Mary Belle describes her feelings:

> I was trying my best to make our apartment a home. I was suffering culture shock realizing that I would never be able to drive a car in this strange place. My feelings were that of being trapped in the apartment. I would look out the kitchen widow at the brown mountains in the distance and find comfort in the verse, ' I will lift up my eyes to the hills…where does my help come from? My help comes from the Lord, maker of heaven and earth.'

Meanwhile, every day Chaplain Timm was driven to work by an Iranian driver. The Chaplain wore a civilian shirt over his uniform so as not to draw attention to his being an American soldier. His job was to minister to all American military personnel in the country - Army, Navy and Air Force. They had arrived in Tehran in August. By Thanksgiving the talk of revolution was heating up. The country was put under martial law. Gun shots could be heard in the city. The American government offered to fly military dependents to a safe area. Chaplain Timm had decided that the family must leave. Families could choose to go to Germany, Spain or the U.S. Mary Belle and Shelly chose to come home to Seattle where two of their children were living.

Chaplain Timm remained in Tehran in the apartment which he now shared with some other American officers. As tensions continued to rise, Harry began to sell off some of the household items he felt he could do without. Mary Belle tells of one incident that put her husband on edge. One day an Iranian wearing a Khomeini Guard armband came to the apartment and asked to buy some of their tools. When Harry would not agree to sell, he became angry, shook his fists at him and declared that in a few days it would all be his anyway. He announced that he would return that night to deal with him. Chaplain Timm spent the night with his hunting rifle at his side. He said he never closed his eyes.

A short time later the situation deteriorated. Our military personnel were ordered to evacuate, taking only what they could carry in one suit case. Chaplain Timm chose to bring out only a quilt that was treasured by Mary Belle. Other than that, they left behind all they owned.

THE MIDDLE EAST AND BOSNIA CONFLICTS

By the late 1980s Saddam Hussein, dictator of Iraq was making claims that certain Kuwait territory properly belonged to Iraq. Even though Saddam was blustering openly and moving his troops, it still came as a surprise to most of the world when he invaded Kuwait in August of 1990. In a swift attack, he took the Kuwaiti oil fields, occupied Kuwait City and massed his troops on the southern Saudi Arabian border. The Saudis and Kuwaitis asked for American assistance. America had limited assets in the area at the time but responded by announcing that the invasion could not stand. Shortly thereafter a major air-lift of troops and equipment was underway. Additional supplies and equipment quickly followed by sea.

EARLY-BIRD TROOPS ARRIVE FOR DESERT STORM

Chaplain Imo Smith

Free Methodist Imo Smith arrived with her Army unit in September of 1990, in preparation for the coming war. The arrival of the American troops marked the first time we had placed large numbers of our armed forces on Islamic soil. Saudi Arabia would become the staging area for most of the troops and their equipment. This was where Chaplain Smith was sent to minister.

Because Saudi Arabia was the keeper of Islam's most sacred religious sites, the Saudis were extremely sensitive about the presence and practice of Christianity and Judaism on their soil. In a letter dated October 26, 1990, Chaplain Smith notes that they were not allowed to have open religious meetings with our soldiers and no cross could be worn on the chaplain's uniform. Before they deployed, they were informed that they would not be wearing a cross on their uniform because it was a safety issue for chaplains in an Islamic country. However, when they arrived in Saudi Arabia, it became clear that the real reason for the removal of the uniform cross was that it offended the Saudis. In deference to the Saudis, the American government had agreed that the chaplains would remove their crosses. This was done, apparently, without conferring with the religious bodies who endorsed the chaplains to the military.

When the news concerning the removal of the cross from the chaplain's uniform reached the religious bodies that had endorsed them, there was an immediate backlash. This writer attended a meeting of Endorsing Agents in Washington, D.C. who condemned the decision and expressed their strong opposition to the Chiefs of Chaplains and heads of military services. After a short time, the decision was reversed and the chaplains were again allowed to wear their crosses on their uniforms.

According to Chaplain Smith, she and other military chaplains had total freedom in ministering to their troops, but were warned not to speak of their faith or to give Bibles or other religious literature to the nationals. "Our military worship and Bible studies and prayer times were well attended," said Chaplain Smith. Anxieties were high in anticipation of the coming conflict which resulted in added spiritual interest.

Chaplain Donald Zimmerman

IN DECEMBER OF 1990, DON had completed his readiness training for deployment. His bags were packed, his family prepared for all possibilities, even his death. Ann Marie, his wife, was given full power of attorney so she could conduct legal business in his absence. Taking a few sermons, a selection of worship materials and, just in case, some resources for funerals and memorial services, he then joined his Unit as it departed for the Middle East. It was December 30th, when his 35th Tactical Fighter Wing flew out to Shaikh Isa Air Base, Bahrain. He would remain there for 183 days while the 35th joined other air units in conducting the air war against Iraq. On Bahrain, Air Force, Navy, and Army chaplains ministered to their individual units and dodged the Scud missiles Sadaam launched their way Because of the extreme demands of the war and the long hours required of the troops, Chaplain Zimmerman noted that little counseling was requested.

Unlike the chaplains in Saudi Arabia, the chaplains on Bahrain were not required to remove crosses from their uniforms. Worship services and Bible studies were well attended, with a variety scheduled. Services were offered for Catholics, Protestants, Pentecostals, Seventh-Day Adventists, and Latter Day

Saints. Chaplains constructed their temporary chapels and office furnishings from scrap lumber. Don writes about purchasing an electronic hymn player, public address system and computer locally. Religious publishers were contacted and they responded by donating Bibles and religious literature.

In his Desert Storm End-of-Tour Report, dated 25 July 1991, Don added this warning to his many helpful recommendations:

> All those who are deployed must be physically capable of doing hard manual labor such as filling sandbags, making shelters, pitching tents, setting up facilities, performing buddy care, and spending hours walking the flight line doing visitation. Those unprepared for the harsh demands of combat ministry jeopardize the survival and ministry of the whole chaplain section.

Chaplain Zimmerman would return to the Middle East in 1995 to the Riyadh Air Base in Saudi Arabia in support of Operation Southern Watch. This Operation, which continued until the beginning of the war in Iraq, was conducted for the purpose of keeping an eye on Saddam Hussein from the air.

Chaplain Herstel Carter

IN MID-JANUARY, 1991, THE MARINES began moving north toward Kuwait, preparing for a possible chemical attack. During this time of preparation, Chaplain Carter provided pastoral care for his troops through continuous visitation, conducting of outdoor worship services, and leading small-group Bible studies and prayer times. Using Psalm 91, he found this scripture a powerful message to his troops who faced the unknown. The passage begins,

> *He who dwells in the shelter of the Most High*
> *will rest in the shadow of the Almighty.*
> *I will say of the Lord, 'He is my refuge and*
> *my fortress,*
> *My God, in whom I trust.'*
> *Surely he will save you from the fowler's snare*
> *and from the deadly pestilence.*
> *He will cover you with his feathers*
> *and under his wings you will find refuge;*
> *His faithfulness will be your shield and rampart.*
> *You will not fear the terror of night,*

> *nor the arrow that flies by day,*
> *nor the pestilence that stalks in the darkness,*
> *nor the plague that destroys at midday.*
> *A thousand may fall at your side,*
> *ten thousand at your right hand,*
> *but it will not come near you....*
> *If you make the Most High your dwelling...*
> *then no harm will befall you;*
> *no disaster will come near your tent.*
> (Psalm 91:1-10 NIV)

Probably no scripture ever spoke so profoundly to our troops as they prepared for battle than this Psalm. This ancient promise would come true before their very eyes in only a few short days. On February 22nd, Chaplain Carter states that the Colonel of his artillery battalion, 30th Marines Second Division, called a meeting of his leadership at 6 p.m. He announced the coming date and time of the ground war and urged his leaders to "make peace with God" because of the potential dangers in 30,000 American troops facing 400,000 Iraqi soldiers.

On the evening of February 23rd, the Marines were in position to begin battle. On this solemn night, Chaplain Carter set out to visit his troops once more. The battle was to begin at 0001 (12:01 a.m.) on February 24th. The chaplain tells what happened next. According to Carter, he walked over the mountain and down the other side, observing his compass bearings and counting his steps in case it was dark upon his return. After reaching his destination, meeting with the Colonel and visiting with the troops, he began his trip back to his tent. As he walked along, he again used his compass and counted his steps.

However, at the base of the mountain, he realized he could not see because of the darkness. He did not know which direction he should turn. Carter got down on his knees and prayed, asking God to guide his path so that he would not go the wrong way and fall into the hands of the enemy. As he arose from his knees, he noticed a light all around him. "I was frightened and feared it was the Iraqis, but as I looked around, there was no enemy or friendly troops anywhere. The light was provided by God." As he looked at the ground he could see his shadow. That shadow became his guide. He followed it across the mountain and as he arrived safely at his campsite, the light went away. It was again so dark that he could not see his hand in front of his face. He says of the experience, "It was obvious that God had been my light and my salvation. Indeed, I had walked in the shadow of the Almighty."

That same night, the war began. The battle was fast and furious, Our troops broke through the Iraqi lines and on the third day, the largest tank battle in history took place on the desert. American forces totally dominated the battlefield and Iraqi soldiers began to desert and surrender in large numbers. Also, on the third day of battle, the Iraqis began to withdraw from Kuwait. The war ended on the fourth day. America had lost 148 troops and the Iraqis had lost 100,000 in Kuwait alone, with 300,000 wounded. Chaplain Carter's Marine unit suffered only one casualty. General Norman Schwarzkopf accepted Saddam's cease fire. Kuwait was again free but Saddam was still in power. He would be a source of future trouble.

Bosnia

AS THE DESERT STORM WAR ended, a new conflict was just beginning as old Yugoslavia began to break apart. Croatia, Bosnia, and Slovenia declared their independence. The Serbs were at conflict with the Croats and each was in conflict with the Muslims. It became clear to the world that the Serbs and Croats were engaged in ethnic cleansing. They were killing the Muslims and driving them out of the towns and territory in which they had lived for years. As Muslims huddled together in refugee camps, the U. S. military began to assist them with humanitarian aid.

When the marketplace massacre occurred in Sarajevo in 1994, killing 68 innocent people and wounding over 200, NATO made a decision to begin selective bombing of Serb positions. U. S. planes were engaged to patrol the skies and attack targets. This military operation, ordered by President Clinton, demonstrated our determination to oppose ethnic cleansing, protect the Muslims, and avoid a wider war. Over time, the Serbs came to respect the NATO and American power and determination, and signed a peace agreement to end the war.

This conflict is worth careful study by those who tend to see military power as always destructive. In this case, it seems clear that the limited use of military power did indeed avert a wider war where the outcome would be anyone's guess. It is also worthy of note that America protected the rights of the outnumbered Muslims. Several Free Methodist chaplains played supportive roles in this conflict.

Iraq and Afghanistan Wars

FOR AMERICA, SEPTEMBER 11, 2001, changed a smoldering terrorist threat into a raging fire. That fire coalesced in the bombings of the cities of New York and Washington, D.C. which left America deeply shaken. It was now clear that our government had had enough and would strike back hard. From

E. Dean Cook

2001 to 2003, our military chaplains were a part of the massive build-up in preparation for a terrorist war in the Middle East and around the world.

Afghanistan was the first target because the 9/11 terrorists had planned and trained for their deadly deed in Afghanistan. It was also believed Osama Ben Laden, who inspired them, was hiding there. Later, Iraq became a potential target because it was believed Saddam Hussein had weapons of mass destruction. Since he had already invaded Kuwait and gassed the Kurds, if he did have the weapons there was a good chance that he might use them on us or his neighbors.

In 2003, the United States massed 100,000 troops in Kuwait, placed major Naval assets in the Arabian Sea, and assembled a large number of our air assets in surrounding friendly Arab countries. On February 18th of 2003, we invaded Iraq, smashing our way to Baghdad as Saddam fled into hiding. In a few more days, the Iraqi government had fallen. American troops relaxed and slept in Saddam's palaces. It appeared to be a great victory, but in time, it turned into a quagmire of seven long years of tough fighting. As of this date in 2009, America has endured 4,325 dead and over 31,000 wounded. Many of our finest warriors have returned home without arms and legs and thousands remain scarred emotionally. All the military services have sacrificed but the Army has sacrificed the most, with over 70% of the casualties. The Marines, who fought some of their toughest battles in their long tradition, however, have also paid a heavy price.

Chaplain Mike Burgess

DURING THE PAST SEVEN YEARS, nearly all of our Free Methodist chaplains – active duty, reserve and Guard – have been deployed into the combat zone or in other places in support of the war on terrorism. Army Chaplain Mike Burgess provides us with a vivid picture of his experience as he flew into northern Iraq early in 2003. Along with his airborne battalion Burgess jumped into the combat zone. Before they jumped, however, Chaplain Burgess offered this prayer:

> Almighty God, we bow before you and ask to be weapons of your justice in defeating these evil forces that have visited death, misery, and fear on the people of the earth. Be with us, God, when we leap from our planes into the dark sky and descend in our parachutes into the midst of an unfamiliar land. Give us wills of steel and courage of warriors as we seize arms for battle. The armies of our enemies are unpredictable, Father; grace our arms to meet and defeat

them in your name and in the name of the freedom and dignity of all people. Let our enemies who have lived by the sword turn from their wicked ways so that they might not perish. May their hearts melt in the face of conflict and give up their spirit to fight. Let the battle be swift and our losses be none. Help us to serve you gallantly, be humble in victory, and give you everlasting honor.

The following are his own words about that experience:

> The 173rd ABN BDE, our parent brigade, arrived in Aviano [Italy] on 24 March 2003 a couple days before the combat jump. I spent a few days prepping my equipment and talking to soldiers. I made sure I checked on each group of soldiers. I offered prayers and encouragement. Most people were grateful for the ministry. Some tolerated it. I only had one person get angry with me. My battalion commander asked me what I meant when I said, 'How are you doing?' He was pretty agitated. I just kept walking and just told him, 'I was checking on the soldiers.' Evidently the combat jump weighed on him and other concerns. Moments later he laughed it off. I don't think he realized my intent.
>
> I personally felt the pressure of a combat jump. I had to jump without my assistant. This is not a good thing but I felt I needed to be with soldiers if anything unfortunate happened. One of the sergeants, Sergeant First Class Lauer, asked me, 'what was wrong.' He told me, 'Chappy, it is like any other jump till you reach the ground.' This lightened my spirit and helped me to focus on the mission.
>
> The brigade spent some five hours on a C-17 airplane getting ready to jump into Bashur, Iraq. I could see many concerned faces and many relaxed faces. Within an hour of getting to the objective we hooked on our rucks. Minutes from the objective the red light came on. We hooked up our parachutes and prepared for a jump of a lifetime. When the green light went we started going to the door. I felt like a pop can being thrown out of a moving car except I had a parachute. The arrival to the ground came early and I landed in the dark of night in a plowed field with nothing broken or bruised and much of this from my wife, Sandra's prayer for a safe landing. She did anytime I jumped.

The battalion landed with just minor injuries and Chaplain Burgess credits God with having heard their prayer.

Chaplain Victor Toney

VICTOR TONEY, CHAPLAIN USAF, HAS served five deployments apart from his family at this writing, two of them to Iraq. He was on his third pastorate when Dr. Kline, our Endorsing Agent, called him, saying he had an opening for an active-duty chaplain in the Air Force if he so desired – he could take two weeks to decide. Driving to Wilmore, Kentucky, to seek God's guidance, he ended up in the writer's driveway. We talked at length about the opportunities of the chaplaincy and I urged him to apply. Next, he contacted Rex Carpenter who was stationed at Nellis Air Force Base. Rex also encouraged him to take the orders. Vic took the leap of faith, applied for active duty and has become one of our finest chaplains.

He writes of one of his rare experiences in Iraq:

> I probably have been one of the few, if not the only chaplain, who has ever conducted a jointed Christian-Muslim memorial service in Iraq. An aircraft with four Americans and one Iraqi went down. One of the pilots, an Iraqi, had attended our worship services in Kirkuk. When it was decided to do a memorial service for all who lost their lives, I had the opportunity to craft a memorial service that did just that;…uplifting Jesus Christ, acknowledging the Christian faith of the Americans [and] the Muslim faith of the Iraqi pilot. Many Iraqi dignitaries attended, including the head of the Iraqi Air Force.

At the present, Chaplain Toney serves as Staff Chaplain, Plans, Programs, and Personnel for the Air Force Command at Wright-Patterson Air Force Base.

Chaplain Stephen Coates

NAVY CHAPLAINS HAVE THE OPPORTUNITY and challenge of ministering to what may be the most diverse settings of all the military chaplains. Chaplain Stephen Coates' career reflects this great diversity. He has served the Navy, the Marine Corps, and the Joint Special Forces, at sea and ashore. It seems that every new assignment requires that he adjust to a whole new setting. During the Iraq War, Stephen received orders to the Joint Operations Task

Force as an "Individual Augmentee". He was required to undergo special training so that he might enter the silent world of these elite forces known as "operators".

These special warriors have forged a strong bond with each other through years of training and dangerous operations. It would not be easy for a chaplain, an outsider, to penetrate their world. However, through prayer, personal encounter, as well as the posting of scriptures and conversation on their portal bulletin board, Chaplain Coates was successful in gaining acceptance. By doing so he was able to enter the most closed community in the world. He was successful in engaging their minds, their hearts and their wills, spiritually.

Coates shares a powerful story of his ministry that began in Iraq but continued all the way to the VA hospital at Bay Pines, Florida:

> I prayed with an unconscious young Army Ranger who had been wounded with a gun shot to the head at close range. His chances of surviving the flight from the field hospital in Iraq to the regional medical center in Landstuhl were about fifty-fifty. I comforted his friends as they struggled with potential loss.

Later, in the States, Chaplain Coates, while in Washington, visited the Ranger recovering in Walter Reed Hospital. His story continues:

> I visited him, though I would never have recognized him from our first encounter. He could not speak but he was beginning to write a few words on paper. I met his mother. You can imagine her tears when I told her I was with her son in Iraq when we flew him out of the war zone. She was overwhelmed with gratitude that a chaplain was by her son's side in his hour of greatest need.

Sometime later, Chaplain Coates was attending a conference in Tampa Bay and visited the nearby VA hospital to see his wounded Ranger again:

> I took my chaplain's assistant with me to visit this remarkable young man, now scheduled for cranial reconstruction surgery. For now he wore a helmet to protect the caved-in left side of his head. Through an amazing progression, this young man was now able to speak with us. His young wife was at his side and once again I had the privilege of praying

for this Ranger. Never again will I question whether God has me where he wants me. I will simply endeavor to serve where I am placed. And why not? I'm telling you it's the greatest job in the world.

Chaplain Richard Winchester

SOME MILITARY CHAPLAINS BECOME SEASONED through the experiences they face after becoming a chaplain. A few become chaplains after they have already been seasoned. Rick Winchester represents the latter. When I first met him he was already a First Sergeant in the Army, having transferred to the Reserves in order to follow a call to the ministry. He and his family chose to attend our church while he pursued his studies at Asbury Seminary. They were clearly leaders and were greatly loved by the congregation. An even stronger bond was forged when their teenage daughter was diagnosed with bone cancer of the leg. She underwent surgery and several months of treatment at St. Jude's Children's Hospital in Memphis. This required extended stays by her parents at the Ronald McDonald House. The treatment was successful and she has gone on to live a rich and productive life. Their experience and their testing of faith was a true lesson in church love, as well as demonstrating the mature faith of Rick and Lesa.

When Rick graduated, he returned to North Carolina, his home conference of the United Methodist Church, to pastor and seek ordination. It soon became clear that his theology and ministry practice were more in line with the Free Methodist Church than with the United Methodist Church. When he inquired about ordination in our conference and possible endorsement to the Army chaplaincy, I strongly recommended him to our conference Ministerial Education and Guidance Board. The Board voted overwhelmingly to accept him for ordination and endorsement to the chaplaincy. Things moved quickly because he had already built an excellent record of Christian leadership and zeal for the Lord.

Rick was brought on active duty by the Army and it was not long until his duties took him to Afghanistan, Uzbekistan, Kuwait, Qatar, and Iraq. He ministered at considerable risk to himself by traveling the dangerous roads all over Afghanistan including the road from Bagram to Kabul which the Russians named the "Highway of Death". In addition, he ran the road from Kuwait to Baghdad with his troops, serving the soldiers in the Green Zone as they secured the area after toppling Saddam Hussein.

During this period of maximum stress on our troops, Rick walked among his flock, encouraging them and bringing to them a sense of God's presence when all else seemed chaos. According to Rick, in addition to the trauma of battle and constant sniper fire, troops were sometimes subjected to more stress when they had time to call home. When a crisis did arise on the home front, Chaplain Winchester was often called upon to help resolve the situation. Sometimes the distress posed danger to the individual soldier and sometimes to the unit itself. Winchester shares some of these conflicts that called for the chaplain's quick action

> I had to deal with taking ammunition and weapons away from distraught soldiers. We had a young private in the 22nd Signal Brigade. His Lieutenant called me and told me to meet with the soldier because he had just learned that his wife was having an affair. These soldiers were smart, they had learned how to read their wife's e-mail. He had read his wife's e-mail and discovered she was having an affair with another soldier who was assigned to his battalion and was flying into Iraq to join the unit today. The private was volunteering to go pick him up. I had to go and physically take his ammunition away from him on the spot. He didn't resist the chaplain.

If someone other than the chaplain had confronted the soldier, there could well have been violence.

Chaplain Winchester tells of another case where he was called upon to talk a soldier out of acting in violence toward his superior:

> We had a couple of cases where soldiers threatened to kill their commanders. It gets down to one or two things. 'You are either going to give me the weapon or I am going to take it. If I have to take it, it's not going to be pretty.' As I told my soldiers, 'It's probably going to be a 'laying on of hands session' and it's not the kind the Bible talks about.'

The chaplain had credibility because the troops knew that he, as a former soldier, had walked where they walked, and felt their pain. They also knew they could not con him because he could back up his words with actions if necessary. Because of the high regard in which they held their chaplain, Winchester could be a pastor, a friend, a drill sergeant and a father to them. Some times he needed to be all four in one day.

A special duty Chaplain Winchester was assigned, as were many of our chaplains, involved preparing a religious assessment of the culture, society and political situation in which our troops had to operate. This may seem strange to Americans who live in a culture where people tend to keep their religious beliefs separate from their public life. However, in Muslim countries, their religious/spiritual beliefs permeate their social, tribal, and political life also. Therefore, the chaplain becomes critical in interpreting these religious values and beliefs to our soldiers who must interact with the culture. This critical and delicate area may hold many risks for the chaplain. If the chaplain should over step his/her boundaries and be seen as a gatherer of military intelligence for combat operations, he/she would lose their rights as a non-combatant under the Geneva Convention. This is a vital issue on which the Church and the military needs to have an on-going dialogue. The very institution of the chaplaincy could be at risk if the lines become too blurry.

Chaplain Winchester found his soldiers ready to talk with him about family, children, hopes, dreams, fears and faith. He described them as young adults on a journey to discover themselves and the meaning of life. There is no greater harvest field for the chaplain and his message. The troops need and want a chaplain with them. "No matter what the press said," Winchester wrote, "the Iraqi's wanted us there. They brought us gifts." Rick's guiding scripture has been Proverbs 27:17, *"As iron sharpens iron so one man sharpens another."*

Chaplain Samuel Cabrera

SAM CABRERA HOLDS THE DISTINCTION of being the first Hispanic Free Methodist military chaplain and the first to come out of the Bronx in New York City. Chaplain Cabrera was educated at Anderson University and Gordon-Conwell Seminary. He entered the military chaplaincy through the Vermont National Guard. Later, he applied for, and was accepted into, the Army. Since entering the chaplaincy he has served at Ft. Hood, Ft. Campbell, Ft. Knox, and is presently Installation Chaplain at Ft. Stewart and Hunter Air Field in Georgia. In addition, he has served in Korea, Alaska, Bosnia and Afghanistan.

One of Sam's special gifts is creating and leading Gospel services. Through these warm-hearted, Bible-centered worship services, he has seen many soldiers come to the Lord and grow in their new-found faith. Presently, at Ft. Stewart he leads the Gospel service which is the largest worship service on the installation.

While in Afghanistan, Cabrera ministered in support of NATO's Operation Enduring Freedom IV. In the course of his duties he traveled throughout the country, at great risk to himself, in order to bring Christ to his troops and to supervise his younger chaplains. During this time, Chaplain Cabrera participated in the first-ever interfaith prayer breakfast with Afghan mullahs. The content of this service and its location must remain secret because of the sensitive nature of the Islamic country.

Chaplain Kurt Spond

"I love my job," says Chaplain Kurt Spond. He goes on to say:

> Often the conversation starts with, 'We don't know where else to go', or 'This is a last stop in an attempt to fix….' Whether it's a marriage in rubble, suicidal thoughts, or just another crossroad in life that forces them to seek advice, they come to the chaplain's office. I don't know how many marriages have been saved in my office. I do know that I spend a large portion of my day rebuilding marriages. I don't know how many suicides have been averted. But I have helped many men place a life that they felt was without value on a foundation of hope. And I can't tell you how many family and friends I have brought the comfort of Christ to in times of despair and loss. What I can tell you is the opportunity lies before me to keep being that "earthen vessel" that holds that hope of the Savior as long as I have breath….I was a soldier before I was a follower of Jesus Christ. When God called me to Seminary, I told him that I thought he had the wrong guy. He told me to shut up and move out. So in obedience I went, confused, to Seminary. As soon as I arrived I ran into Bob Barnard who asked me the simple question, 'Have you thought about military ministry?' Of course! God does have a plan. And what a great plan it is.
>
> Once I knew where I was going, I was able to find a great mentor in Chaplain Cook. As a pastor, he helped me mature. By sharing his military experience with me he helped me prepare for the transition into the Army a second time even though he's a bit partial to the Navy.

Kurt transferred from another denomination into the Free Methodist Church while in Seminary. To gain practical experience as a pastor, he took a small congregation near Crab Orchard, Kentucky. He and his wife, Mary, were a great encouragement to this congregation he helped save and which now flourishes. Once an Army sergeant, Chaplain Spond has made a smooth transition back into the Army and is doing an exceptional job. He shares this heart-warming story:

As I was preparing to leave my office for a lunch meeting... he came into my office and asked if I had time to meet his family. When he introduced his wife she said to me, 'So you're the guy!' He replied, 'He was there.' In Kuwait, just before we moved into Iraq, the soldier had told me with great pride that he was an atheist. Since he was the son of a preacher he was well-versed in church-speak and ready with stories of the hypocrisy that he had seen. We had many pleasant conversations over the course of the next twelve months on church, creation, politics, etc. Most of these conversations were during combat patrols south of Bagdad or in a small patrol base that his company occupied. I would spend about two days at a time with them and then move to the next of my four patrol bases on my circuit. We had a relationship that old soldiers are familiar with, formed in combat. It's a 'Hooah' thing.

Near the end of the tour, my soldier friend's worldview failed him. As his marriage unraveled he started seeking answers and I was there. More importantly his Savior was there. He and his wife are now doing great, repairing their relationship. They were both baptized this April. He has three more years on his enlistment but he's already thinking about coming back as a chaplain.

Chaplain Mark Williams

ON FLORIDA'S EAST COAST, JUST below Cape Canaveral and Cocoa Beach, sits one of our nation's most important military bases, Patrick Air Force base, home to a space wing command that launches military satellites and rockets to keep us safe. On a recent visit to Patrick to attend the retirement of our Air Force officer son, Scott, a member of the Space Command, we were honored to meet one of our outstanding young chaplains, Chaplain Mark Williams. Mark, who is from Florida, had come home to minister in this very important and closed community.

In 2007 he had deployed as senior chaplain of the 506th Air Expeditionary Group, 332nd Air Expeditionary Wing, in support of operations in Iraq. Chaplain Williams had already distinguished himself by writing a book on The Character and Core Values of the Air Force. The Air Force published the book and distributed it to all new officers entering the Air Force. While in Iraq he also designed and led a form and style of worship for his troops that was highlighted as a model for others to follow. He also initiated a reintegration program using retreats and workshops to assist his troops in strengthening their marriages.

One particular relationship he developed stands out as remarkable:

> I met an Iraqi Kurdish pilot while stationed at a forward-operating base. He was an instructor pilot for the newly-form Iraqi Air Force. Disillusioned with many things, he showed up at our worship service to see what the Americans did. After attending several services and counseling sessions, he was baptized on Christmas Day.

It is a joy to see our new generation of chaplains distinguishing themselves as bold servants of Christ early in their ministry. Their actions prove that they not only sense how the Spirit works but that they also are willing to be used of Him in closed communities under sensitive circumstances.

Chaplain Anthony Randall

ACCORDING TO OUR RECORDS, CHAPLAIN Randall is the first Free Methodist chaplain to hold the distinction of being a West Point graduate. In 1996, he graduated from the Military Academy as a Second Lieutenant Engineering Officer, and served from 1996-2001. At that time he left the military service and began his own consulting business called Vanguard XXI which provided leadership consulting, team building, and management training to businesses, as well as to academic and religious institutions. He published his first book in 2002 entitled The Vanguard Factor.

By 2002, God had called Anthony to full-time ministry and training at the Denver Theological Seminary. It was here that he became a Free Methodist and sought ordination with the Rocky Mountain Conference. After serving as a pastor for two years he returned to active duty as an Army chaplain in 2006.

The Surge Operation that finally secured Baghdad and allowed the President to set a withdrawal date for our troops from Iraq, was a major turning point in the war. Chaplain Anthony Randall was a part of that Surge during his fourteen months in Iraq. During this period he served as Squadron Chaplain for the 3-1 Cavalry Squadron. Most recently Chaplain Randall has done ground-breaking work on strengthening the soldier against the possibility of PTSD. As a part of his doctoral dissertation, he has written a training exercise entitled "The Resilient Warrior" which we referred to in Chapter Six, "The Veterans Administration Chaplain".

Chaplain Charles Roots

> I had my first brush with death in combat. A mere thirty minutes after landing at Danang, Vietnam, we were hit by a rocket attack…a piece of shrapnel struck me square in the chest as I was diving for cover. I reached down and picked up the hot piece of metal, and have kept it to this day….

Charles Roots went to Vietnam as an enlisted Marine. Following the war, he left the Marines and responded to a call to ministry. Soon after completing seminary, a Navy chaplain recruiter contacted him and suggested he should consider entering the Navy Chaplain Corps. He and his wife prayed about the matter for several months, and concluded this was God's will for them. Upon completion of the Chaplains Basic Course, Chaplain Roots was assigned duty again with Marines at Camp Pendelton.

His follow-on duty was aboard the supply ship WHITE PLAINS (AFS 4), home ported out of the island of Guam. While serving aboard WHITE PLAINS, Charles recruited and trained a clown team of six sailors which performed as a ministry to children at the various ports they visited throughout the Pacific. This creative effort was extremely effective and was written up by several military newspapers, as well as the Stars and Stripes publication.

In 2003, Chaplain Roots was sent to Djibauti, Africa, to provide ministry to a counter-terrorism base:

> In all my years of ministry, I have never been so privileged to see the hand of God at work as I did there. The base was a multi-service, multi-national mix of Special Forces from all branches of the service, along with various military representatives from a host of other nations, all in support of the War on Terrorism.

When Roots arrived at the base, he discovered he was following a chaplain who had been lacking in the performance of his duties. Because of the chaplain who preceded him, Chaplain Roots faced the monumental task of winning the support of his Marine Commanding Officer. However, it was not long until Roots had developed a practical and visionary strategy for ministry that impressed his commander.

He began by creating a supportive program to a nearby baby orphanage run by Roman Catholic nuns. This effort by base personnel became so popular that the chaplain was required to run two van loads of volunteers a day to the orphanage. The military volunteers included all ranks from

Chaplaincy: Being God's Presence in Closed Communities

privates to colonels. Two other orphanages, for older children, were also located nearby. Again, the chaplain recruited and coordinated volunteers to teach the children athletics and play games with them. In addition, they also taught English classes At the same time, the chapel program grew rapidly, requiring eight separate religious services be conducted weekly, not including Bible studies and prayer meetings.

One of the most effective and creative ministries came about during the Christmas season. Again, service members volunteered to write and act in a Christmas drama to be produced at the chapel. The proposal received the chaplain's full endorsement:

> To give you an idea of what these folks had to work with, the guys who played the Roman soldiers, wore their desert combat boots, fashioned broad swords from packing material….Sheets were used for body clothing typical of that era and region. The baby Jesus was a child's doll, the star of the East was cardboard wrapped in aluminum foil from the mess hall, attached to a stick and carried across the stage behind a tarp curtain…lighted by a flashlight.

The drama was crude; in fact, the chaplain said it could have even been considered "hokey" but it proved to be a powerful presentation of Christ's birth under the circumstances. When it was performed at the chapel, this child-like drama, played by tough military personnel, received a standing ovation.

Since the General was away at the time, upon his return he heard about it and requested it be performed again, for him and his invited guests, which included delegates, dignitaries and diplomats. Again, following the presentation, the drama team received a standing ovation from their distinguished guests, come of whom were Muslims. The Catholic Bishop of Somalia/Djibuati, invited the team to present the drama at his cathedral. "No one," recalls Chaplain Roots, "least of all me, could have planned this or anticipated the amazing response. This was God at work."

Chaplains can often find themselves in what may seem at first a God-forsaken place, but when they exercise faith and vision, great things can happen, to the glory of God. Chaplain Roots retired in the rank of Navy Captain after twenty-five years of service – eleven years active and fourteen reserve.

The Chaplain's Spouse

It is impossible to end this chapter on the military chaplain without giving recognition and honor to the chaplain's spouse. In many cases, especially where there are children involved, these heroines deserve at least as much honor as those who go. No other spouses of ministers are asked to sacrifice as much as these. After a difficult deployment ends and the troops come home, no one pins a unit citation, or bronze star, or purple heart on their chest. No one gives them a promotion or an assignment to a better job. In fact they may well be expected to repeat the whole process again and again. These are the real patriots who deserve to be honored alongside their chaplain mates.

Conclusion

To conclude this chapter, it must be said that the story of our military chaplains is the story of love for Christ, country, and the fine young Americans who protect our freedoms. They bring Christ to people on the sea, in the air and to the farthest corners of the earth. Their task is daunting; yet they are seldom heard to complain. Instead, their memories and testimonies overflow with gratitude to God for the high privilege of serving.

Chaplaincy: Being God's Presence in Closed Communities

EARLY MILITARY CHAPLAINS
Line 1: Harry Webb, George Whiteman, William Allayaud, Harry Ansted Sr.
Line 2: Owen Mullett, Merlin Probst, Carson Reber, Kenneth Fristoe
Line 3: Bergen Birdsall, Forest Walls, A.W. Darling, Charles Kingsley
Line 4: Robert Hayes, Horatio Ogden, Wesley Robb, Robert Warren

* All the pictures above were taken from the Free Methodist Magazine

MORE EARLY MILITARY CHAPLAINS
Line 1: Francis Fero, George Biddulph, A.R. Harford, Robert Klein
Line 2: Oliver Porter, John Hoyt, Kendall Mahew, Walter Mack
Line 3: Harry Ansted Jr., Clason Rohrer, Roscoe Bell, E.R. Ray
Line 4: Charles Ackley and counselee, Lowell Ronne

* All the pictures above were taken from the Free Methodist Magazine

Chaplaincy: Being God's Presence in Closed Communities

Harry Ansted, Sr. with son Harry Ansted, Jr.

Myron Henry
Navy and Correctional Chaplain,
Association President,
Designed Chaplain's Medallion

Chaplain Randall Tucker
Army and V.A. Chaplain.
Wrote the Association's Constitution
First Association President

E. Dean Cook

Captain Fuchita led the 360 plane attack on Pearl Harbor, December 7, 1941. Sergeant DeShazar participated in the "Doolittle Raid" on Tokyo, April, 1942, in response. Here they meet as Christian brothers in Missionary DeShazar's home in Japan.

Chaplain Roscoe Bell and wife, Betty, entertained Fuchita and DeShazar in their home while stationed in Japan.

Chaplain Dean Cook led in the naming of the new chapel at Pearl Harbor, **The Pearl Harbor Memorial Chapel**, for those who died on December 7, 1941

Chaplaincy: Being God's Presence in Closed Communities

Chaplain Anthony Randall serving communion to his troops in the field.

Chaplain Vic Toney, (left) Air Force

Chaplain Samuel Cabrera

Chaplain Stephen Coates, Navy

CHAPTER FIVE
HOSPITAL CHAPLAINCY

I<small>N THE BOOK</small> <u>A S<small>ENSE</small> of the Sacred</u>, the Health Care Chaplaincy of New York City states the mission of their health care chaplains: "The Health Care Chaplaincy is a multi-faith community of professionals committed to the advancement of pastoral care, education and research. We are dedicated to the spiritual care of all people who suffer in mind, body, and spirit."

Father Damien

T<small>HIS DEFINITION OF A HEALTH</small> care chaplain gets to the very core of this compassionate ministry. People who are not empathetic need not apply. There have been great souls who were led to minister to the suffering long before the health care chaplaincy existed. Today's chaplains stand on their shoulders. One such soul was Father Damien. Having lived in Hawaii twice, I am personally acquainted with his work and have visited the leper colony where he lived. To reach the Molokai colony, one must take the pack mules down the mountain and descend the steep switchback to the bottom. Beginning in the 1800s, Hawaiians who had contracted the dreaded leprosy were torn from their families, and transported by ship to Molokai. Upon arrival, they and their meager belongings were often tossed overboard, forcing these unfortunate souls to swim ashore, to spend the rest of their lives suffering with other lepers.

However, in 1873, a Belgian missionary priest felt led by God to come to the island to care for these suffering outcasts. It is a surprise for some to discover that Presbyterian missionaries were on Molokai long before Father Damien arrived and they had already established a work among these suffering people. But in the minds of the lepers, no one ever cared for them like Father Damien. He identified with their suffering by becoming one with them. This writer visited the colony and the small chapel he built for their worship. Because some could not contain their saliva and let it drip on the floor, or went to the widow to spit during mass, Father Damien simply cut holes in the chapel floor to accommodate their need. It was a small thing but it spoke volumes to the lepers about his sympathy toward their needs. The final and greatest proof of his identification with their suffering came when he contracted leprosy himself.

After his death, the people of Hawaii honored him by erecting his statue in the place of honor at the center of their state capital building. Father Damien left a model for all health-care chaplains to imitate.

Development of the Hospital Chaplaincy

UNLIKE THE PARISH PASTOR WHO visits in the afflicted, as one of several duties demanding his time, the health-care chaplain has only the suffering patient as his/her primary ministry. In carrying out this ministry the chaplain may use religious symbols for reassurance and comfort, such as the Bible, anointing oil, the cross, the sacraments and religious literature. These can all serve to strengthen the patient's mind, body and soul, but the most important sacrament and symbol is the presence of the chaplain and his/her loving touch on the patient's life. It is often then that the love of Christ is the most present, powerful, and healing.

Development of Free Methodist Hospital Chaplaincy

FREE METHODIST PASTORS HAVE ALWAYS cared for the afflicted but many years passed before the Church, endorsed the first health-care chaplains. So, how did the Church's health care chaplaincy begin? Our research seems to indicate that it probably began from two sources. First, our world missions' effort always had a health care component. Early on, we sent nurses and doctors to staff mission clinics, hospitals, and schools. This arm of the Church's missions' program drew our missionaries into the ministry of health-care.

Secondly, our military chaplains were often trained and assigned to duties in military hospitals both on the battlefield and at support bases at home and overseas, For example, Navy Chaplain C. W. Ackley served at the Camp Pendleton Naval Hospital and wrote of his rich experience for church publications. Chaplain Gail Buckley served a tour at the Portsmouth Naval Hospital in Virginia, and Chaplains Ken Carpenter and Dennis Demond both served as chaplains at the Army's major medical center, Tripler Army Hospital in Honolulu. Like the missionaries who served in mission clinics, hospitals and schools, our military chaplains helped pave the way for the Church's growing involvement in hospital chaplaincy.

Records show that in America chaplains began to be added to hospital staffs somewhere in the mid to late 1920s. As time passed, these pastors from ordinary church settings were required to meet a high standard. Like military chaplains they were urged to have a college and seminary degree and be endorsed by a recognized religious body. However, these chaplains differed from military chaplains in that they did not have an age or physical fitness requirement. In addition, they were required to have completed four Clinical Pastoral Care units which translated to about 1600 hours of training under the watchful eye of a Clinical Pastoral Education (CPE) supervisor. Also, many hospitals expected their full-time chaplains to be certified by the Board of the Association of Professional Chaplains. Today there are general hospital chaplains and chaplains who specialize in such areas as geriatrics, pediatrics, AIDS, neonatal – and the field grows.

The hospital chaplain plays a key role in teaching parish pastors and lay persons how to make hospital calls. Untrained pastors or lay visitors can unknowingly harm a patient or cause added stress if the pastor says or does the inappropriate thing. The hospital chaplain's coordination with the parish visitors is not only good patient care but it also protects the hospital against needless law suits. This writer was involved in a case in which a young pastor visited a major hospital to see a parishioner who was having mental health problems. The pastor, untrained in hospital care, commenced to question the patient and pressed her to repent of her sins. The patient became very agitated, and hospital aides rushed to the room to intervene. The pastor was asked to leave. Later, the attending physician called the senior pastor and asked that the young pastor no longer visit the patients.

Hospital Patients

PEOPLE WHO COME TO THE hospital for treatment are under stress and are captive to the hospital care. They did not come to the hospital for spiritual ministry or lectures on their spiritual life. They may welcome all this when they are ready, but the chaplain must approach them carefully and sensitively. The patient may come from one of many faith groups or may have no faith at all. They may even be angry at religion and/or the Church. The chaplain must ask permission to join the patient on their journey of healing. First, the chaplain must become a listener and after trust has been established perhaps they can become an effective intercessor, advocate and counselor in helping the patient clarify, strengthen or lay hold of faith. The patient's family is also a part of the healing process and often needs the chaplain's assistance, counsel, and support. In addition, the chaplain may be called upon to interpret the patient's spiritual and emotional health to their attending physician and hospital staff.

Chaplain Ray Roller, Yavapai Regional Medical Center

WHEN THE WRITER BEGAN THIS chapter, Hospital Chaplain Ray Roller had been admitted as a patient in the hospital at Yavapai Regional Medical Center in Prescott, Arizona where he was employed as a full-time chaplain. At age 88, Ray Roller was the oldest active health-care chaplain in our Church. In semi-retirement, he continued to serve in the position of Chaplain Services Coordinator, a position developed especially for him. Ray had ministered 20 years as a part-time contract chaplain with the Prescott Veterans Hospital. Later, he had been invited by the Medical Center to take their chaplain position in which he served faithfully as senior chaplain for 24 years. A recent heart operation had left him incapacitated. Before he was hospitalized, Chaplain Roller wrote these words:

> I have reached the mature age of 88, but instead of asking me to retire, they employed a new Pastoral Care Director and created a new position [for me] 'Coordinator of Volunteers'....it will require about 16 hours a week. Let me share what our Hospital philosophy is regarding our pastoral care and chaplains. The hospital has a Pastoral Care Advisory Committee consisting of the Hospital CEO, the Director of Human Resources, Director of Nursing, and Director of Volunteers. The chaplains' meetings are attended by this Advisory Committee.

This kind of support from a Hospital Administration is highly unusual and a tribute to the outstanding ministry and leadership of Chaplain Roller. The Vision of YRMC is worth noting because it clearly recognizes a spiritual dimension to their health care:

> The Vision is to create a total healing environment wherein the people of YRMC work in partnership with patients and their families seeking peace of mind and peace of heart as well as physical cures or comfort because we understand the indivisible relationship that exists between body, mind and human spirit.

As in most major hospitals, the chaplain could not begin to provide the scope of pastoral care needed without the help of many volunteer chaplains.

Thus, one of Chaplain Roller's major tasks was to recruit, train and supervise a band of 45 professional volunteers. Most of these volunteers were drawn from the ranks of active and retired clergy. If a volunteer pastor is assigned to a church, he/she is required to attach a letter to their application from their church stating that the church supports the pastor's volunteer hospital ministry. If accepted by the hospital, the volunteer clergyperson must then enroll in the hospital's training program and must embrace the rules and regulations of the hospital. Each volunteer is expected to do three 24-hour shifts a month from 8 a.m. to 8 a.m.

It was with great regret and sadness that we received word since the above communication that Chaplain Roller had passed away in the hospital in which he had ministered for so many years. It was reported that, at his memorial service conducted at the hospital, the administration and staff turned out in large numbers to show their gratitude for the life and work of their "grey shepherd". The Church has lost a great chaplain and compassionate warrior.

Patients' Rights

ONE OF THE CONCERNS WHICH Chaplain Roller expressed before he died was the importance of chaplains and churches understanding the patients' rights. Because of the number of law suits filed against hospitals, it is a growing priority for the hospital chaplains to educate and train community clergy on understanding and respecting patients' rights. Federal regulations regarding patients' rights are now a critical issue for those who minister in hospitals. Most laypersons and clergy calling in hospitals today do not have an adequate knowledge of this federal regulation. For example, patient information cannot be shared with the church or anyone else without the expressed permission of the patient. Much of the information shared in church services, church prayer groups, church bulletins, and other means of communication could be in violation of this federal law, if patient's clear permission was not granted. This is a serious matter because it changes the way in which the Church, clergy and Christian communities have traditionally operated.

Chaplain Ben Belcher, Harrison Memorial Hospital

CHAPLAIN BEN BELCHER (RETIRED Navy chaplain) has been the Director of Pastoral Care at Harrison Memorial Hospital, Bremerton, Washington, for twenty-eight years. Ben has had excellent training in health care, having completed five units of Clinical Pastoral Training. Ben shares his calling to the hospital chaplaincy:

> In my senior year of college, I felt the leading of God to go to seminary. I did not feel a particular lead to be a pastor... As one of my elective classes I decided to take a unit of CPE through Lexington Theological Seminary at the University of Kentucky Medical Center. I was assigned to the cancer ward and, while many patient situations were heartrending, the ministry was wonderful. At the time I did not know the impact it had on my life.

He returned to his home conference and was assigned a church. Three churches later he still did not feel he was in the place that God had chosen for him. He finally decided to make a change. An opportunity presented itself for him to serve in a part-time hospital role. He took the leap. Twenty seven months later a Free Methodist nurse, Ruby Henry, wife of Navy Chaplain Myron Henry, told him about a chaplain position in her hospital and urged him to apply. He did so, was accepted, and has been there ever since. Chaplain Belcher's story is repeated time and time again because the chaplaincy is not always understood or presented forcefully and clearly in colleges and seminaries. Ben is one of the more fortunate ones; he did not give up even when he assigned a ministry that did not satisfy his heart. Chaplain Belcher's long record of fruitful ministry as a hospital chaplain, should serve to give others hope who have not yet found their place.

Chaplain Marilyn Behena, Detroit Medical Center Children's Hospital

CHAPLAIN BAHENA IS A BOARD-CERTIFIED hospital chaplain at the Detroit Medical Center Children's Hospital where she serves as Coordinator of Spiritual Services. How she received her calling is a testimony to God' guidance:

> I received my calling one day in November, 1998, when I heard out of the blue, 'You could be a hospital chaplain.' At the time I was a wife and mother and a directory entry midwife attending homebirths. My mind was occupied with an upcoming birth. I had no thoughts about ministry or working as a chaplain. I wondered what in the world was I hearing. Was God talking to me or was I going crazy?

Marilyn shared her experience of hearing the unusual voice and calling with her pastor. Thank God for the pastor who, like Eli of old, sensed that

God had spoken. Three things had a profound effect on this seeker: (1) He showed excitement for Marilyn and what she had heard from God. (2) He confirmed her calling by telling her that he thought she would make a wonderful chaplain. (3) He suggested that she respond by offering to become a volunteer at the local hospital. Marilyn did respond as a volunteer and then God led her on to Clinical Pastoral Training at Children's Hospital of Michigan. Her call was confirmed through the many experiences she encountered at the hospital with hurting children and parents.

> As time went by my supervisors encouraged me to begin seminary and hired me first to serve as an adjunct chaplain and later as staff chaplain. Finally in 2007, I was asked to take on the role of Coordinator of The Spiritual Care Department, supervising other staff chaplains, adjunct chaplains, chaplain residents, and interns.

Chaplain Behena also brings the advantage of special communication skills to her hospital ministry. She has an earned degree in bilingual education and Spanish. Listen as she describes how her use of Spanish has enhanced her ministry in the hospital setting:

> I thank God for my fluency in Spanish. Thank God for a voice that can sing lullabies in Spanish to calm a frightened toddler with tears rolling from his big brown eyes. Thank God for hands that can pat, arms that can rock, and Christ's heart that can express love to stop terrified tears until a little one whose mother is injured and unable to come from another hospital, finally relaxes and falls asleep in my arms. I praise God for the ways He can use me—I am often able to help Hispanic families who speak limited English and feel completely alone and powerless in the hospital. Sometimes it is as simple as listening to their story and offering understanding. Many times I have interpreted for Spanish speaking families through-out a child's illness so they could ask their questions and understand the diagnosis, treatment plans, and prognosis. I have helped many of these families through multiple surgeries, heart transplants and sometimes the death of their children...laughing and crying, rejoicing and grieving with them Many have limited resources and are sometimes here in the country illegally so they have no insurance. I am the hospital worker who can explain their

fears to the physician and their financial needs to the social workers. I have often been involved in drafting letters to immigration services to bring parent or grandparent from Mexico or Guatemala to see a gravely ill child. I have helped arrange for beloved children to be flown home to Mexico for burial.....I have prayed with families....I have been present many times at a child's last breath and held up parents as they sobbed on my shoulders. I thank God for using my voice and arms, hands and feet to give Christ's love and compassion to the world.

Behena also shares a deeply personal and moving experience she had with Alexis, a beautiful baby girl born with a kidney disease that required doctors to remove both kidneys and most of her intestines. They hoped to find a kidney-intestinal transplant for her. For five months the baby struggled as the parents and chaplain prayed for her survival. Finally the mother sensed that the child would soon die and came to the chaplain with an unusual request. The mother wanted to take the baby outside so she could experience the sunshine for the first time. The chaplain approached the attending nurse and the two of them discussed the matter with the attending doctor. The doctor called the hospital workers and in 30 minutes they were wheeling baby Alexis outside to the Hospital Healing Gardens in a special isolette.

The family enjoyed a special time with Alexis, holding her up so she could see the sun for the first time. It was a beautiful 70-degree day in November, with a soft breeze. As the baby marveled at the sunshine, the mother stroked the face of her child. Together, the chaplain and family experienced something that day that deeply bonded them. The baby's mother later wrote the chaplain, "You will never ever know the extra joy you put in my heart on November sixth. I didn't know dreams come true until I met wonderful people like you."

> This experience with baby Alexis was probably one of the most fulfilling in my nearly ten years of chaplaincy ministry and it became even more meaningful to me six days later when my own father was dying after a two-year battle with colon cancer. The ambulance drivers who were taking him home from the hospital for hospice care fulfilled my father's wish in much the same way we had fulfilled the wish of Alexis' family. They offered to drive him back through bumpy fields to look over the winter wheat of his farm just one more time, after I had asked them to just stop for a

moment along the road. They did more than I had ever asked or imagined, even unloading my father's gurney out of the ambulance into the stubble from harvested corn so he could see the expanse of waving green wheat. My father smiled as he saw the green fields that promised new life the following spring. We all knew that very soon he would be the grain of wheat that would fall to be born again into eternal life (John 12:24). I was so grateful to see his joy at being home on his farm and for the precious moments he had in fulfilling his wish to see the fields where he had labored for 45 years. I was grateful to the kind ambulance drivers whose compassion and mercy literally made the drive off the beaten path to make it possible. My father died the next morning. In the following grief-filled days I felt the echo of Jesus' words, 'Blessed are the merciful for they shall receive mercy.'

Chaplain Behena exemplifies the heart and sensitivity that is required of an exceptional children's hospital chaplain. The Church can be thankful that she listened to the voice of the Lord, and that she had a pastor and CPE supervisors who recognized her rich gifts and encouraged her to enter the hospital chaplaincy.

Chaplain Douglas Burleigh, Bessett Healthcare Center

IN THE EARLY 1990S I drove from Rochester to Cooperstown, New York, to visit Chaplain Burleigh, who was employed at the Bessett Healthcare Center. This fine hospital, located in the beautiful city that is also the home of the Baseball Hall of Fame, was involved in a number of creative health programs. Chaplain Burleigh was the hospital's first and only paid chaplain. This provided him the rare opportunity to develop the position and himself professionally, while integrating spirituality into the hospital's healing mission.

For the next sixteen years, Burleigh immersed himself in this task, providing quality spiritual care to the hospital's patients and staff. He not only developed the chaplain department with creative programming, but also designed and dedicated the hospital's first chapel. Serving as a member of the hospital's ethic committee (which he chaired for seven years), serving as the Hospital's liaison with the Center of Donations and Transplants, and co-chairing the Palliative Care Committee, placed Chaplain Burleigh at the very center of the hospital's leadership.

In the area of public service, Chaplain Burleigh acted as liaison to the community clergy and provided them important training related to the pastoral care of their flock. He was also asked by the Hospital to develop and conduct educational workshops on spirituality for healthcare professionals.

Chaplain Burleigh's contribution to his hospital and community was highly significant because it went beyond the normal expectations of a healthcare chaplain. His leadership and giftedness enabled him to make his hospital more sensitive and responsive to the people they served. It is easy for an institution in its busyness and preoccupation with financial solvency to neglect or overlook the spiritual nature of its people. It is at this very point that chaplains like Chaplain Burleigh can make their greatest contribution.

Chaplain Dwight Sweezy, Trenton Psychiatric Hospital

AFTER THREE YEARS IN THE parish ministry, Dwight Sweezy realized he could pursue two ministries, both of which he felt called to fulfill – the U.S. Army chaplaincy and the mental health chaplaincy in a state psychiatric facility.

As a child, Sweezy loved to accompany his pastor-father on pastoral visits to homes, jails, veteran homes and nursing homes. In Albion, New York, where his father pastored for five years, they lived across the street from the county jail. Young Dwight accompanied his father who held weekly worship for the inmates. These childhood experiences served to remove all fear and anxiety about ministering behind closed walls. When, as a teenager attending a Genesee Conference youth camp, he felt God clearly calling him to the military chaplaincy. Later he joined the Army as a chaplain's assistant and did a tour in Vietnam.

Later, in 1974, after graduating from Asbury Theological Seminary, he did a unit of CPE at Eastern Kentucky State Hospital. There he was assigned to the case of a young 21-year-old woman who had attempted suicide. As her primary therapist, he worked with her for four weeks, seeing remarkable results in her life. He states of this case:

> Her wrists were bandaged where she had cut herself in desperation to relieve her depression. In the course of a pastoral visit to her, I felt impressed to stop my avoidance of her bandages and, gently touching one of her wrists, I asked her if her wounds hurt very much. This question resulted in a flood of tears and her sharing the pain of her life. Until that moment, she thought it only made sense to end her pain and life since she was convinced of her isolation and despair...in the following four weeks we worked together in

her claiming her value, as one of God's own with purpose and future....Through this patient, I learned the value we all have when we join together in our struggles whether physical, mental or spiritual.

From this experience with the young lady at Eastern Kentucky State Hospital, Sweezy felt an even stronger conviction of his call to a ministry of counseling and pastoral care with those who struggled with severe mental illness. Thus, he took a position at the Trenton Psychiatric Hospital while also joining the Army Reserves as a chaplain. He writes, "I know God's presence is very real within the halls of a state psychiatric hospital if one is only willing to broaden one's expectation of this presence looks like."

He shares a powerful story about a female patient, a schizophrenic library in her late 20's:

> I met her when I saw a piece of her coat under a back pew in our hospital's inter-faith chapel during Sunday morning worship. I thought someone left their coat, but upon further focus, I saw her wrapped in one of her three coats under the pew. This went on for a few Sundays. She came early and slipped out before I could greet her at the close of worship. One Sunday during the Passing of the Peace, I leaned down her level and attempted to greet her with a handshake and a 'Peace be with you'. She pulled away. 'Oh, pastor, no please don't touch me. I'm contagious. I don't want you to get what I have.' She was convinced that anyone who might touch her would become mentally ill like her. She couldn't be convinced to join our community of faith, but she loved to attend and from her unique location was a faithful attendee at worship.
>
> Over the months that followed, she slowly began to return to the human race and specifically our fellowship. First, she began to sit on the back pew, then she moved a little closer to the front, next she hesitantly joined the Passing of the Peace, and the most moving day for me was when she came to the altar with others to take communion and her place within our community. Shortly thereafter she was discharged.
>
> Since she has not been hospitalized these past twenty years, it seems that lessons learned and steps taken within an accepting community of faith has been an important

part of her journey toward a healthier life and a return to a productive place in society.

Summing up the satisfaction he has from his ministry in the hospital, he writes,

> I have witnessed and celebrated where those deemed hopeless by others, find hope, acceptance, and meaning even in a state hospital. I have been blessed by knowing and journeying with so many individuals for whom each day is a struggle to survive, a confusing jungle of experiences to manage, and a deluge of emotions to control, yet who still have the courage to try and face the new day. I am certain I have received far more than I have offered.

In addition to Chaplain Sweezy's individual ministry to patients, he manages a heavy load of other responsibilities. For example, he leads a multi-faith and inter-denominational department of chaplains and has provided clinical supervision for over 300 students from Princeton Theological Seminary who come to his hospital for their field experience. In addition, he has been President of the Medical Staff Executive Committee, Chairperson of the Hospital's Bio-Medical Ethics Committee, and a member of the Hospital Cabinet, Chairperson of the Patients' Rights Committee, to name only a few.

Sweezy concludes his description of his ministry by saying, "Each day the challenges and activities of ministry are rewarding, different, and meaning-filled. It is humbling and a blessing to be a part of God's presence with those who are often likened to the lepers of the New Testament stories." Chaplain Sweezy has, and is, making a major contribution to this ministry and to the lives of the severely mentally ill. He is bringing the light of Christ to a dark place because he dared to go minister behind closed walls.

The hospital chaplaincy continues to grow in numbers as the healthcare industry confronts the growing scientific evidence that spirituality plays an important role in the healing process.

Chaplain Ben and Judith Belcher

Chaplain Marilyn Bahena

Chaplain Dwight Sweezy

Chaplain Mary Laverne Jackson with Rex Carpenter

Chaplain Paul and Janice Schantz

Chaplain Daniel and Linda Hummer

Chaplain Fletcher and
Carolyn Simpson

Chaplain Diane Munoz

CHAPTER SIX
VETERANS ADMINISTRATION CHAPLAINCY

The Veterans Administration lists 1865 as the birthday of their chaplaincy. In this year, President Abraham Lincoln signed legislation to establish the first National Home for Disabled Veterans. Provision was made at the same time to assign a chaplain for each National Home. That chaplain was to be paid $1500 per year and forage for one horse. This historical Home is still located in Hampton, Virginia, and is now the site of the National Chaplain Center Headquarters.

Veterans Administration Chaplaincy Development

It was not until 1930 that the Veterans Homes were placed under the control of the Veterans Administration. Local clergy, who ministered only part time, were the first chaplains to Veterans hospitals. The General Commission on Chaplains for the Armed Forces in 1944 saw the great need for ministry to returning veterans and negotiated with the Veterans Administration to take responsibility for providing chaplains. The Veterans Administration was receptive to the idea and after a study appointed Rev. Crawford W. Brown, an Episcopalian, as the first Chief of Chaplain Services.

At first the chaplains were placed under Special Services, the department that provided recreation for the vets, but this was challenged by the chaplains and they were later placed under their own department.

National Chaplains Service

The National Chaplains Service was established with a starting goal of 125 chaplains. A plan was devised to provide a chaplains school for training and to assign a chaplain for each hospital with a minimum of 500 beds. In the late 1940s, General Omar Bradley, then the Veterans Administrator, directed the new Chaplain Director to start placing chaplains in Veteran Hospitals. By 1953 the VA employed 262 full-time chaplains and 280 part-time. In 1983, the first female chaplain was appointed as Director of VA Chaplains. Over the years the Chaplain Directors have been appointed from a variety of faith groups. The number of chaplains employed has varied over the years due to budget restraints and demands, but the number has remained around 400 full time and 200 part time.

Like the military, the Veterans Administration has been sued over mixing spiritual care with medical care at government expense. The opponents of the VA chaplaincy argue that spiritual ministry is intrusive into the lives of the patients. They say the patients are too vulnerable and open to persuasion during their illness. Although some suits are in progress as we write, most veterans and their families clearly want the presence of the chaplains and feel that spiritual ministry is a part of their healing process and civil rights.

Free Methodist VA Chaplains

VA CHAPLAINS MEET A HIGH standard for pastoral care. They are well trained, and have their own Clinical Pastoral Education certification. Presently, the Free Methodist Church endorses five full-time VA Chaplains: Dan Hummer, Paul Schantz, Jon Wright, Rob McLaren, and Bruce Swingle. Lael Dixon (recently retired) and the late Randall Tucker, also served in the VA for many years. Other pastors and retired chaplains, such as this writer, continue to minister as chaplain volunteers in their local VA hospitals..

Early VA Chaplain Harry Webb

CHAPLAIN HARRY WEBB, ONE OF our Army chaplains, became a Veterans Administration chaplain following WWII, at the VA Hospital in Dayton, Ohio. He was one of our earliest VA chaplains. An article written by Chaplain Webb appeared in the January 1957 issue of the Light and Life Magazine. It is accompanied by a photo of him serving communion in the Dayton VA Hospital tuberculosis ward. Chaplain Webb draws us a poignant and heart-moving picture of a VA chaplain's day:

> He struggled to swing one crutch ahead. One foot could be moved ahead easily, and he balanced himself rather precariously as he swung the second crutch forward with a wide sweep. Then he pulled the other foot along without difficulty. I greeted him and he said to me, 'Chaplain, it

seems like I am a thousand miles from home.' He had moved about 200 feet! He glanced up at some gathering clouds and asked, 'Do you think it will rain today?' – he seemed to be calculating the time it would take him to return to his quarters. Farther on I met a man vigorously manipulating his wheelchair as though he was anxious to get to his destination....across the street I heard the familiar tap, tap, tap of a white cane, giving evidence of the pathway to its darkened owner. I went into the building and conducted service as planned. It was a mental ward and men could hardly participate vocally or mentally. Therefore, the leader had to do most of the singing. A patient made his way into the room in a wheelchair. His muscles made a half dozen movements before making the one he wanted, and then immediately started on another series of random movements. He managed to get where he wanted, however, and while he was doing so the thought came over me that I was doing for him what he could not do for him. He wanted to worship God, or he would not have struggled with all those muscle movements to be present, but the chaplain made the expressions of worship available for him. I cannot help but think of the scripture that speaks of the 'poor, the maimed, the halt, the blind.' What a privilege to help them worship God, and to point them to Him in the hour of need. No gratitude ever came from the heart more deeply than their words, 'Thank you, Chaplain!' No vocal chords ever struggled more sincerely to make available an expression of appreciation. The chaplain's day is filled to overflowing in ministering to these 2,000 aged and handicapped veterans – calling on them, praying with them, encouraging them, leading them in worship, and helping them find God.

Chaplain Paul Schantz, Augusta VA Medical Center

NEW SOUTH CONFERENCE MEMBER PAUL Schantz has been serving at the Augusta, Georgia, VA Medical Center for thirteen years. He and his wife, Janice, are outstanding examples of our dedicated VA chaplain families. Paul also graciously agreed to act as a primary resource and consultant on the writing of this chapter, for which he deserves a special thanks.

Under the preaching of Pastor (later elected Bishop) Donald Bastian, Paul went forward at Greenville College and said a final yes to God. After college he enrolled in studies at Asbury Theological Seminary but was unclear as to how God was specifically leading him. Following graduation, Paul took a church in rural Georgia near where his sister and her husband, Brian Bonney, were pastoring at the time. Over the next few years, Paul pastored several Georgia and Alabama churches but struggled over a lack of church growth. Following his assignment to the Huntsville, Alabama church, Paul talked with Bishop Clyde Van Valin about his sense of failure in the role of the parish pastor. The bishop suggested he enroll in CPE classes. "I didn't know what the letters meant," Paul writes. However, in 1993 he enrolled in the CPE program at Carraway Methodist Medical Center in Birmingham, Alabama. He describes his experience in CPE training:

> While at Carraway, a real change began in me. I learned that grace was wider and more welcoming than I had ever known, even though I had preached it for many years. I began to understand God's love in a more profound way... The CPE supervisors used some vocabulary I thought unnecessary. My thought was, 'Real Christians live higher than that.' Many of my fellow residents found it liberating to use some of the same language. But, interestingly, I found in them (the students) a genuine desire to know God's grace! One supervisor had a short fuse. I was the focus of it a time or two in good CPE fashion. Earlier he had invited me to a Tuesday night basketball scrimmage. One evening the supervisor and another student got into an angry shoving match. I grabbed the arm of one and another student grabbed the Supervisor and the game resumed. The next morning I was called in to see my Supervisors. The Supervisor who had been in the tussle had confessed to his Supervisor and his integrity demanded that he apologize to me for his not having set a proper example. Grace!

Paul goes on to say that while at Carraway he came to understand for the first time that chaplaincy ministry was the same grace as pastoral ministry. He now saw that the message and the grace was the same for both. At the end of his CPE training, he felt free to pursue applications for the chaplaincy. First, he took a half-time hospice position in northern Alabama, then a contract chaplaincy at the Augusta VA Hospital. In 1998 he was selected for a full-time position at Augusta after being honored as the VA Contract Chaplain of the Year, a high honor that I'm sure did not go unnoticed by his selection committee.

Changed by CPE Training

CHAPLAIN SCHANTZ SHARES WITH US how he was profoundly changed by his CPE experience and how that change affects his VA ministry today:

> While at Carraway, the senior CPE Supervisor proposed an idea. He stated that each of us has a dominant emotion out of which we live: mad, sad, glad, hurt, or afraid. After some thought I concluded that I lived out of hurt and fear most of my life. It is not easy living hurt and scared. Tozer reminded me that, 'We live under friendly skies'....I do not know when it happened, but at some point in a three-month period, I recognized I was living in joy. It has seemed to be my dominant emotion since. It has also been the theme of my ministry with the veterans. It does not matter where a veteran has been or what they have done. The God of heaven wants to be the friend of all.... I find an almost universal truth in the verse by Fanny Crosby, 'Down in the human heart, crushed by the tempter, feelings lie buried that grace can restore. Touched by a loving heart, wakened by kindness, chords that were broken can vibrate once more.'

Ministering to a Paranoid-Schizophrenic Veteran

ONE PARTICULAR PARANOID-SCHIZOPHRENIC VETERAN COMES to Chaplain Schantz's office often. His thought processes are all but impossible to follow. His language is earthy, his dreams will never come true, but before he leaves the chaplain's office he wants to have prayer. "The man's prayer is genuine and from the heart," says Paul. Commenting on his friend, he goes on to say, "It is my joy that he has a safe place to relax and knows I am his friend. With me he is in the presence of the Holy." Chaplain Schantz also has a ministry to those with dementia. Their language may also be salty, their outbursts unpredictable, yet he states that, "When I invite them to pray with me, there is a change in demeanor....They go into a quiet place with God where, for a few moments, there is peace and fellowship with Him. The best thing I can do as a chaplain is to take them with me into the presence of the Holy."

A Substance-Abusing Veteran

A YOUNG VETERAN HAD LEFT his family and his community in shame after a life of substance abuse. He entered the Veterans Substance Abuse Program and found the chaplain a welcoming friend. Accepting the chaplain's invitation, he joined a spirituality class. Over time, the man saw what he had become and what he needed to be. Through a new relationship with Christ, this poor soul was transformed. Like the man Jesus healed, his neighbors were amazed at the change they observed in him. With joy, peace, and enthusiasm, he now tells them that the Lord transformed him. This is just another example of why the VA believes that chaplains and the spiritual care they provide is a vital part of their healing process.

VA Coverage in State of Georgia

ACCORDING TO PAUL, GEORGIA HAS three VA hospitals - in Atlanta, Augusta, and Dublin. This is probably typical for most states of similar size. Chaplain Schantz writes, "To improve access to care, over the last decade the VA has changed from a hospital-based system to include an out-patient-based focus. It is estimated that veterans made more than 60 million out-patient visits to VA health care facilities across America in 2008."

Some 300,000 returning veterans from the Global War on Terrorism have sought the VA health care services. Serving the veterans nationally are 153 hospitals, 732 community-based out-patients clinics, 232 veteran centers, 135 nursing homes, 47 residential rehabilitation treatment programs and 121 home care programs. The VA is the most comprehensive health care network in America.

In the following paragraph Schantz discusses the VA chaplain's ministry and his/her place in that healing community:

> The VA has always recognized that the care of the body alone cannot be effective if the mind, heart, soul and spirit are ignored. The chaplain, as part of the health-care team, is the one that addresses the spiritual needs of the veterans. Often when it is most needed, an illness isolates a veteran and /or family from the community support of home. The chaplain does not replace the local religious leaders but fills the role of being a spiritual friend away from home. The chaplain is able to point to grace that can make a new way of living a viable option for someone trapped in addiction or other health problems. Veterans come from all parts of a multi-cultural society. Each patient has a fundamental right to considerate care that safeguards personal dignity and respects his or her cultural and spiritual values. VA Chaplains are trained for such ministry...Most chaplains

are certified by The Association of Professional Chaplains or the National Association of Veterans Affairs Chaplains.

Chaplain Daniel Hummer, Bay Pines VA Medical Center

HE IS ONE OF OUR longest-serving VA chaplains and has also served in top leadership positions in the Chaplains Association. Chaplain Dan Hummer has been one of the strongest advocates for our Church's chaplains.

A few years ago, Chaplain Hummer invited our Association Executive Committee to meet at his residence in Largo, Florida. During our time together, he arranged to take the Committee on a tour of the Bay Pines Medical Center where he worked. It was a rare opportunity to observe Dan as he made his rounds on the wards and in the units. We were surprised to discover that he was affectionately known in the hospital as "the singing chaplain". Because of his love for music he had taken to singing hymns and spiritual songs to the staff and patients as he went about his normal calls. They responded with delight and often joined him in singing. It was a wonderful thing to behold as we saw how his songs had the power to literally change the whole atmosphere on the wards and in the spirit of the people. It caused some faces to brighten and smile and brought a joyous note into the midst of a suffering community.

Chaplain Hummer had found an effective and non-threatening way to enter into the human hearts through songs of the heart. Why should we be surprised at this therapy of singing when we remember that Jesus sang with His disciples at the Last Supper and Paul and Silas sang at midnight in the Philippian jail? Chaplain Hummer's unique ministry is just another example of how a positive spiritual ministry can change the tone of a workplace.

Chaplain Jon Wright, San Francisco VA Medical Center

SOME VA CHAPLAINS HAVE NEVER served in the military. Some have served and gone on to become VA chaplains. But only a few have served as VA and military chaplains at the same time. Jon Wright is one of the few. While serving as chaplain in the San Francisco VA Medical Center, Wright also served as chaplain in the Army Reserves, rising to the rank of Colonel before recently retiring. At this writing, Chaplain Wright continues to serve the VA in the San Francisco area.

One of Wright's duties is to visit veterans at the downtown VA outpatient clinic. Many of these veterans are homeless, suffer from substance abuse, and struggle with mental illness. He confesses that when he first visited the clinic, which was located in the rough part of the city, he felt a sense of fear. The fear was soon dissipated when the veterans and staff welcomed him with open arms. The chaplain writes of his experience:

> One of the veterans said he would watch out for me, and each day when I would go to catch the bus back to the hospital, he would accompany me to the bus stop and stay with me until I was safely on the bus. One time a homeless veteran took me to his shack nearby, which was under a large freeway complex, and invited me into his abode, constructed mainly out of tarps, cardboard, and wooden planks. As I came to know these veterans and visited with them and prayed for them, and became more familiar with their illnesses and personalities, my fears melted away. One veteran who has schizophrenia, has a deep and profound belief in and love for Jesus and he is an avid student of the Bible and fervent in prayer. When off the proper medications, he can become very paranoid and angry. However, he never loses his humility before God, his desire to confess and repent, and his recognition of his need of the Holy Spirit constantly in his mind and heart. He doesn't have much in a material nature in his life, but he has a very grateful attitude for God's daily presence, protection, and power. Many of these veterans say that the weekly visit with the chaplain and participation in the spirituality group, and receiving the sacraments of communion, is one of the most important ingredients in their lives, as they live and cope with illness, addictions, poverty, and spiritual attacks.

In addition to his ministry to the outpatient clinic, Chaplain Wright also ministers at the VA hospital. The following is an account of one of his ministry opportunities:

> At the VA hospital, I was visiting a veteran in the intensive-care psychiatric ward. He had very bizarre behavior and was a handful for the staff– often they had to put him in the isolation room and at times…restrain him…on a mattress. He had been open at times to visiting with me and never threatened me. One time he let me know that he was so afraid of evil and the devil that he needed all the spiritual power from all the religions of the world. One time when I

visited him…he was lying on his bed but he recognized me and invited me in. "Chaplain, pray and anoint me," he said. I anointed him with oil and prayed for him in Jesus name. He didn't say anything else but was very still and quiet. Next week when I came to the unit, the staff commented how totally different he was in his mood and behavior, now being very calm and cooperative in his behavior. He came to our worship service on the next Sunday and as I played the hymns tears streamed down his cheeks. From that time on he would always greet me with a big bear hug.

These stories reflect the needs of our veterans and their openness to spiritual ministry. Chaplain Wright continues the tradition of true spiritual worship in our VA administration.

Post-Traumatic Stress Disorder

WE NOW KNOW THAT THE strains and trauma of war are deep and often lasting. In years past it did not escape notice that our warriors who came home from the war often chose not to talk about their experiences and sometimes felt it difficult to relate to others. People respected their silence but had little understanding of the pain and deep questions that this silence masked. Most were left to suffer alone. Today, because of our troops' repeated tours in the combat zone, an unusually large number of them are suffering from PTSD. The military health-care system and the Veterans Administration are now giving high priority to the study and treatment of this illness. PTSD is the brain and body's response to overwhelming stress such as being shot at, seeing your fellow soldiers wounded or killed, or being wounded yourself.

The symptoms of PTSD can include an inability to sleep, nightmares, angry outbursts, depression, suicidal thoughts, flashbacks and substance and family abuse. These symptoms can last for weeks or years or suddenly surface after a number of years. Families can be affected deeply. In such cases the whole family may need treatment and counseling.

Several of our Free Methodist chaplains are playing key roles in helping develop material for the training and treatment of PTSD wounded warriors and their families. Related injuries are also TBI (traumatic brain injuries from concussions) and COS (combat operational stress). Free Methodist Chaplain David Thompson, USN retired, and Licensed Professional Counselor, has done extensive work with the military in Minnesota. As a counselor, he has worked with a mental health team on contract to the military in support of the Minnesota National Guard's "Beyond the Yellow Ribbon" deployment cycle support system. Their work with the National Guard has provided a model that has been a resource throughout the military service and the VA.

Thompson and a colleague were invited by Abingdon Press to co-author a book based upon their experience that would help churches minister to service personnel and their families under this mental stress. The book will soon be in production and is entitled <u>Beyond the Yellow Ribbon: Ministering to Returning Combat Veterans</u>. David's interest in this subject has recently increased, as his own son, a newly-commissioned Army officer, has received orders to the Demilitarized Zone between North and South Korea.

Chaplain Anthony Randall, US Army, has written a study curriculum related to PTSD entitled "Operation Resilient Warrior" as part of his doctoral studies and thesis. His work has received positive recognition at the highest levels of the Army. Chaplain Rob McLaren, one of our Free Methodist chaplains serving at Bay Pines VA Hospital in Florida, (along with Chaplain Dan Hummer), has created an excellent packet and program to assist families and individuals that suffer from PTSD. It speaks well of our Free Methodist VA and active duty chaplains that they are at the forefront of this critical battle to help heal our wounded warriors.

While writing this section, I rode an Amtrak train from Indianapolis to Chicago. Soon after leaving the Indianapolis station, a man in his sixties, seated nearby, engaged me in conversation. He told me he had been to the VA hospital in Indianapolis for treatment of PTSD. In our discussion, it became clear he knew a lot about the illness. For the next hour, he told me his story.

As a young sailor aboard the USS Forrestal Aircraft Carrier during the Vietnam War, he had experienced the devastating fire on the flight deck which engulfed (now Senator) John McCain's aircraft along with others, leaving several hundred sailors dead and wounded. Because of the threat to the ship, the engineering spaces below were sealed off. This man and others who worked in these engineering spaces found themselves trapped below deck, unable to escape. After several hours of being sealed off, the fire was finally brought under control and the doors and hatches opened. At the time, this man felt he had successfully dealt with the trauma and his life returned to normal. That is, until Senator McCain ran for President in 2008. During the presidential campaign, the Forrestal fire was widely revisited in the media. As the man repeatedly watched and listened to these accounts, it triggered the emotion, fear and anxiety he felt years before. Eventually, it developed into the debilitating illness of PTSD where he could no longer function in his job. He sought treatment at the Indianapolis VA hospital. The VA caring community he found was helping him regain control of his life again. This program, like others sponsored by the VA, has chaplains assigned and helps to restore wounded warriors to full health. It seemed to me Providential that I should meet this man at the very time I was researching this subject.

Our VA hospitals are often underfunded and under attack, but they are no less critical to the health of our veterans. The unique healthcare they provide has a significant inherent spiritual element that only a chaplain is trained and equipped to provide. The VA is a rich field for ministry. If a full or part-time position is not available, this writer would urge pastors and ministerial candidates to offer themselves as chaplain volunteers. They will receive excellent training, participate in a satisfying ministry, and enjoy a warm welcome from the veterans.

CHAPTER SEVEN
HOSPICE CHAPLAINCY

WHAT IS HOSPICE AND WHAT does a hospice chaplain do as a member of the team? Who are the Free Methodist hospice chaplains and where do they serve? This chapter will seek to answer these and other questions.

Dr. John M. Finn, Director of Hospice of Michigan, has written an excellent article on "Why Hospice?" It was first published in the Oakland County Medical Society Bulletin in 1989 and was reprinted by Hospice of Michigan. Dr. Finn writes:

> Hospice is the positive solution to the euthanasia debate.... The usual conversation goes like this, 'Doctor, Can you just give me something to put me out of my misery?...we treat animals better than this.'...However, once the same patient has achieved an improved degree of symptom control and once emotional concerns are adequately addressed, the conversation changes to expressions of gratitude and the desire to make the most of the time remaining. Hospice is an alternative to euthanasia. Legalization of voluntary euthanasia poses many potential dangerous social consequences. The right to die would soon become the duty to die. Patients would choose euthanasia because they were becoming particularly burdensome rather than for individual reasons...Most hopelessly ill patients express the desire to die without excessive medical intervention and preferably at home – if support and the support and resources they need are readily available.

The doctor defines hospice as "a medical option when care is not realistic and palliation and comfort are the goals of treatment." The chaplain is an important part of the hospice team. One chaplains said, "Death is the ultimate faith journey....I consider myself a midwife to the dying." The hospice chaplaincy is a part of a growing movement toward healthcare specialization. Although nearly 70% still die in rest homes and hospitals, a growing number are choosing to die at home.

Four hospice chaplains live in and work out of our small Kentucky town. Two of these are Free Methodists - Diane Munoz and James Demaray. Chaplain Munoz graciously consented to write a general history of the Hospice movement and ministry. for this chapter.

Chaplain Diane Munoz, Hospice of the Bluegrass

DIANE IS A MEMBER OF the New South Conference, and is a gifted chaplain, Christian leader, and speaker. She was elected Secretary of the Free Methodist Chaplains Association in 2009 . Her excellent history of Hospice that follows is a good and helpful window into this unique ministry which has brought comfort to so many.

THE HISTORY OF HOSPICE:
THE ART of DYING WELL.

THE WORD HOSPICE COMES FROM the same root word as the terms "hostel" and "hospitality". The root includes a nuance of serving, taking care of others, entertaining (a modern concept), providing housing and even Christ's body – as the divine Host. In the early church the apostle Paul challenged believers to pursue hospitality; in fact, hospitality was a qualification for leadership in early Christian communities. The writer of Hebrews reminded readers to offer hospitality to strangers for, like Abraham and Sarah, they might be entertaining angels. Christian believers were to regard hospitality to strangers as a fundamental expression of the gospel. Jesus promised that welcoming the stranger, feeding the hungry person, and visiting the sick were acts of personal kindness to the Son of Man himself. (Christine Pohl, <u>Making Room: Recovering Hospitality as a Christian Tradition</u>, Grand Rapids: Wm B. Eerdmans, 1999, 5)

The first known hospices were places or respite for weary medieval pilgrims. Some of the oldest hospices, created by physician-monks and nuns, trace their lineage back to the year 1000 A.D.

> The hospice infirmary was an essential part of an institution where travelers also fell sick and died. Within the relatively

safe walls of European monastic communities, the West thus created its first hospital and health care system. A library of records still exist that refer to a larger tradition popularly called the 'ars moriendi', or the art of dying. (Richard Groves, <u>The American Book of Dying: Lessons in Healing Spiritual Pain</u>, Berkeley: Celestial Arts, 2005, 13.)

In Beaune, France today is a structure from the 14th century that captures the essence and spirit of these early visionary Christians who walked out Christ's command to the poor, sick, and dying in a way that honored Christ: L'Hotel-Dieu, or God's Hotel. The writer has chosen to expand on its description as, in a very beautiful way; this place and the people who were its members exemplify hospice care at its best. This chaplain desires for her care of patients and their families to somehow embody this spirit of caring and compassion and, frankly, beauty.

The only measure of a society's greatness depends upon how it cares for the poorest of its poor at the end of life.
Nicholas of Rolin, Founder of l'Hotel-Deiu

The Hospice de Beaune was conceived in the mid-fifteenth century only a few years after France's patron saint, Joan of Arc, was burned at the stake. During Europe's bloody Hundred Years' War, the lot of the average peasant was desperate. Roving bands of murderers, rapists, and extortionists spread terror through the countryside, as one of Europe's most devastating plagues decimated entire populations. Life and death for the average person was brutish.

> In the midst of this despair, the region's chancellor, Nicholas Rolin, convinced both king and pope to exempt the newly constructed Hotel of God from all taxes in perpetuity. The result is a masterpiece of civic Gothic architecture that rivaled the palaces and cathedrals of its day. Rolin and his wife, Guigone, created a prestigious foundation nicknamed "the palace for the poor." They employed some of Europe's great artisans to decorate the roofs with polychrome tiles and emblazon the walls with luxurious Italian commissioned Flemish painters to create one of the best-known altarpieces of the time. Instead of a grim asylum for the dying, this hospice provided luxurious attention for the sick and dying that rivaled the lifestyle of royalty.

Beaune's extraordinary architectural and artistic achievements are only an external expression of the more important work that was housed within. Inside, a small army of nurses and volunteers tirelessly supported the physical and spiritual well-being of the dying. Word was soon out all over Europe about a new standard in health care at the end of life.

A medieval artist's rendition of the l'Hotel-Dieu gives a fifteenth-century vision of the end of life with the creative imagination of an entire community at work. The picture's title, *La Grande Salle des Povres en Dimanche Matin,* translates as "The Great Hall of the Poor on a Sunday Morning."

This hospice did not serve the privileged nobility of the day, rather it was dedicated as a hotel for social outcasts.

The artist depicts a flurry of activity, including townspeople providing Sunday brunch, nurses nursing, children playing, musicians singing, and even pets bringing familiarity and solace. The caption could read, 'It's Sunday morning, and where is it happening? At the hospice.'

In the painting there is a liturgical prayer being conducted at the far end of the building which was unusual for this period. After all, this was not a house of worship but a secular community hospital. Every dimension of care giving is interconnected. The core belief of this hospice model was that care for the body necessarily involved caring for the soul.

Architects still marvel that the elegant hospice complex was built over a River, with a glass floor underneath patients' beds. This unique feature enabled the sick and dying to hear the soothing sound of water, enhancing the environment for patient and care giving alike. Each private cubicle was furnished with a bed and, more marvelous for the day, clean linens, table settings, a complete apothecary, and aesthetic refinements otherwise available only to royalty.

There were not more than two patients per bed in a time when three or four were common in the hospitals. Thanks to the canopy and the curtains the beds formed a closed cell protecting from the cold. Behind the beds were chests for the clothes of the patient. Upon arrival the patient received a bath and their hair was cut. They would put on the clothing of the hospice with their own belongings being disinfected with sulphur, placed in the trunk, in the event they would get well and leave. The patient went to confession; a clean body and a clean soul were critical to care received. The chapel was there to remind of the spiritual dimension of healing along with a polyptych of the Last Judgment upon the decorated altar.

Looking upward at the ceiling and rafters…, [one could] read the mantra of the ancient hospice movement: *'Ars sacra moriendi, ars sacra Vivendi.'* **The sacred art of dying is the sacred art of living.** Here at God's Hotel is a five hundred year old image of the West's finest hour in caring for the terminally ill. For the fifteenth-century residents of Beaune, the dying were indeed their teachers. (www.virtualtourist. com/travel/Europe/France/Bourgogne/Beaune-136180/ Things_To_Do_Beaune-BR-1.htmi, November 16, 2008, 15-16.

*Dame Cicely Saunders Ignites Modern Western Concept of Hospice

The Hospices de Beaune were the last great expression of the original Western Hospice model. By the year 1492, modernity was about to be born with all the benefits that surround us on a daily basis, especially those in regard to medicine.

By concentrating exclusively on the physical aspects of care giving, Western medicine would eventually lose its centuries-old instinct concerning other matters/issues at the end of life. Care for the sick and dying was about to become institutionalized and professionalized, as family, neighbors, and friends abandoned their own inclination to support others at the end of life. The notion of diagnosing and addressing spiritual pain would become disassociated from the treatment of pain and disease. Since 1492 a crisis management model of illness had become the norm in the West. (Ibid, 16)

The fact is, we are all terminal; we will all die. Current American culture has done a solid job of repressing our thoughts about death, leaving many without the tools to die well. A survey done by the Last Acts, a national coalition to improve health care for the chronically ill, found that 83% of Americans state they would prefer to die at home. Currently, 75% of us die in nursing homes or hospitals. Despite advances in medical technology, Dr. Ira

Byock, the first president of the American Academy of Hospice and Palliative Medicine, found that, in general, the last two generations of Americans have not died well.

> Americans spend more money on medicine and high-cost care at the end of life than any other society in history. Physicians now have an arsenal at their disposal to control physical symptoms like breathlessness, nausea, and pain. Yet for many of us, at the moment of death, something essential is missing. (Ibid, 2)

Clinicians in the spiritual care field, as well as an increasing number of medical professionals, believe the answer to that dilemma is in the soul-sized questions that typically show up in the nearing death experience.

Thankfully, there was a lady born in England who also saw the connection between soul and body as one nears death. This English pioneer and physician (actually a nurse, social worker and physician), enabled extraordinary work in the field of death and dying. Dame Cicely Saunders, (1918-2005), established St. Christopher's Hospice in London, challenging the perception that people had to die in agony. As a result of her vision, the modern hospice movement created a realistic hope for a future in which nobody has to die alone or with pain untreated. (Ibid, 19) Today, St. Christopher's welcomes 4,000 visitors annually and more than 50,000 health care professionals from all over the world have trained there.

At a time when many embraced euthanasia, Dame Saunders had a different viewpoint. Her vision led to a model that has changed the face of dying across the world. Among her legacies was the gift of the concept of "Total Pain Management". Saunders questioned practitioners' fear that their dying patients would become addicted to medications. Rather than respond to pain with intermittent sedation, Saunders' novel method of pain control provided a steady state in which a dying patient could remain conscious and maintain a good quality of life. However, she did not confine pain relief to the physical. The concept included physical, emotional, social and spiritual elements. She focused on caring for the whole person and enfolding their family and friends within that care. This led to the development of a new medical specialty, palliative care and modern hospice philosophy.

> ***You matter because you are you, and you
> matter to the last moment of your life.***
> *Dame Cicely Saunders*

*Hospice Comes to the United States

Today, in the United States, the word hospice is synonymous with care to the terminally ill. The western concept of Hospice care came to the U.S. via a nursing dean at Yale University. *Florence Wald* was Dean at Yale Nursing School. Her interest in compassionate care for the dying led her to launch the first hospice program in the U.S. She introduced the concepts of a stronger focus on comfort care for dying patients and their families in the 1960's within the nursing school curriculum. Mrs. Wald's passion for hospice was sparked when she heard a lecture by Dame Cicely Saunders, the founder of St. Christopher's Hospice in London. Mrs. Wald organized the Connecticut Hospice in 1974 in Branford, widely accepted to be the first U.S. hospice program. Mrs. Wald more recently worked to bring hospice care to U.S. prisons and to train inmates as hospice volunteers.

*Hospice Chaplain Practice in the United States

Today, 35 years after the first hospice formed in the United States, there are some 4,000 programs nationwide that focus on providing care for terminally ill patients and their families. Together they serve about 900,000 patients each year. Hospice gained more use and attention after Congress ordered Medicare in 1982 to start paying for the service. Most hospices employ nurses, social workers, home care aides, chaplains and bereavement counselors. While there is still a wide-held notion that hospice is for cancer patients, cancer patients account for less than fifty percent of hospice diagnoses. Among the other qualifying terminal illnesses: End-stage heart disease, End-stage renal disease, Chronic Obstruction Pulmonary disease (COPD), failure to thrive and debility unspecified. While patients are required to have a physician verify a prognosis of six months or less to live, anyone can make a referral to hospice: the patient themselves, family member or friend.

Dame Saunders was quoted as saying, *"Spirituality is the most overlooked factor in pain relief."* The role of the hospice chaplain is to lean into that pain. The Celts had a term for those who come alongside the dying to relieve their pain, an *anamcara*, or soul friend of the dying. This writer likens this role to that of a spiritual midwife, enabling persons to come to terms with their spiritual issues at the end of life, thereby enabling a peaceful death, or "birth", if you will, from this life to life eternal.

One of the tools for getting to that pain is a spiritual assessment. In essence, we are asking a series of questions to help us better understand what the person's soul issues may be:

How are things within you?
What do you find yourself thinking about when you lay down at night?
What is giving you life and energy right now?

What regrets might be stealing your peace of mind?
Tell me about your experience of God. Has that changed since your terminal diagnosis?
How do you hold blessing and brokenness in your relationships?
What dreams keep you alive?
How do you sustain hope knowing that you will die?

Most spiritual pain can be broken down into four categories: meaning, forgiveness, relatedness and hope. How is the person relating to themselves, others and God? What is giving them meaning in light of an inability to do physically what they once did? Are there any outstanding reconciliation issues? How might you as chaplain enable that reconciliation? Where do those with seeming no hope, find hope?

Most hospices in the United States are secular organizations that embrace an acceptance of all spiritual expressions including Hinduism, Islam and Judaism. They rightly expect their chaplains to support patients and families in their faith tradition. Therefore, a question often asked in interviews is: "Do you see your role as one to convert and evangelize all your patients?" The chaplain needs to carefully consider how they respond to that question.

In the service area in which the writer is employed, the great preponderance of patients are from a Judeo-Christian background. However, my role as chaplain is to explore where there may be deficits in their spiritual beliefs as they face the final days of their life. What do they believe will happen to them when they take their final breath? To the extent the patient elicits appropriate responses, the chaplain is free to explore their openness to the gospel. As the writer continues to wrestle with her role and integrity as a chaplain, the verse from Matthew 25 informs,

> *Come, you who are blessed by my Father, take your inheritance, the kingdom prepared for you since the creation of the world. For I was hungry and you gave me something to eat, I was thirsty and you gave me something to drink, I was a stranger and you invited me in, I needed clothes and you clothed me, I was sick and you looked after me, I was in prison and you came to visit me. Then the righteous answer him, 'Lord, when did we see you hungry and feed you, or thirsty and give you something to drink? When did we see you a stranger and invite you in, or needing clothes and clothe you? When did we see you sick or in prison and go to visit you?' The King will reply, 'I tell you the truth, whatever you did for one of the least of these brothers and sisters of mine, you did for me. (verses 34-40, NIV)*

Another role of the hospice chaplain is to help educate the patient and family as they approach death. What are the spiritual signs and symptoms? What does it mean when they reach with their hands and arms, seemingly into space and call out to deceased loved ones? What do we make of their visions of seeing loved ones or Christ and the conversations we may overhear? What does the family need to do in preparation for their final departure from this life? Often it is very important for the patient to hear from their families that permission is given to leave or die. This is a final act of tough love to let their loved ones know, that as hard as it may be to imagine life without them, they will be OK and it is alright if they take their final breath. The moment of death can be a very sacred moment and the hospice chaplain is privileged to be a part of that space and to help facilitate what the hospice movement calls a "good death".

- **Educational Requirements for Hospice Chaplains**

While requirements vary greatly from hospice to hospice, the movement is toward all chaplains being board-certified from the APC: Association of Professional Chaplains. To be board-certified a chaplain must have a Masters of Divinity or equivalent degree, be ordained and endorsed by their denomination, and have successfully completed four units of Clinical Pastoral Education (CPE) from an accredited organization. Upon completion of the fourth unit of CPE, chaplains must work another year, full-time, at an accredited organization. After completion of the above, the chaplain candidate can begin the board-certification process which requires extensive verification of work completed, writings related to APC standards and philosophy of care and interviews/examination by a board of APC-certified chaplains. For additional information, consult the APC website at: http://www.professionalchaplains.org/

> *The only people prepared to live,*
> *are those who are prepared to die.*
>   *Henri Nouwen*

With this excellent history of Hospice, let us now hear from some of our Hospice chaplains who are out in the field.

Chaplain Fletcher Simpson, Horizon Home Care and Hospice

IN 1995, WHILE WORKING AT a Christian camp in Wisconsin, Fletcher Simpson met Chaplain Paul Schantz who was then transitioning into the chaplaincy and spoke positively of it. Paul had taken CPE and spoke about his experience to Simpson. In 2001, Chaplain Simpson enrolled in CPE classes in hopes of following in the footsteps of his father, who had been a chaplain at Heritage Village. Upon finishing CPE, he was offered a job at the Home Care and Hospice facility. The hospice ministry at first held little attraction because he had always envisioned himself ministering where he could win souls. Hospice didn't seem to be that place. However, after several months in the work, Simpson began to see that this was the place God had chosen for him. He spoke of how he came to discover this truth:

> I became the chaplain to a 96 year old lady who was a good Christian but had several things she had not learned or dealt with in her walk with the Lord. It amazed me some days how God directed the prayers I shared with her. He was helping this dear lady deal with her disappointment and to forgive a pastor and congregation she felt had abandoned her when she fell ill. I had the privilege of baptizing her by immersion when she was 98 and serving her communion on several occasions. On one occasion she invited her nurse and social worker tocome to her home and take communion with her. This was an opportunity to clearly witness of her faith to the nurse and social worker.

Chaplain Simpson shares another story about an angry patient whose heart was softened by God:

> Then there was Jerry. When I first met him he was an angry man and said, 'So you're a chaplain. Well, I want you to know God screwed me.' I wondered if he was watching to see how I would react to such a statement, but I soon realized he was just being clear with how he felt. He told me of years of struggle in his marriage, with his sons and with his finances. He had just resolved a bitter divorce, and was dealing with the death of his ex-wife. His boys were still struggling, but it was getting better. The one thing that, as we say, 'broke the camel's back' was that he had always dreamed of restoring two old cars. He had been able to find and buy the two he had dreamed of and they sat in his garage just waiting his loving touch. Then he went to the doctor and found that he had cancer and it was advanced and progressing rapidly. He was told he had six months or less to live. This left him no opportunity to work on his 'dream' cars.

> After a couple of visits he shared some of his spiritual understanding and that he had not been interested or concerned about that before. I prayed God would help me find a way to make clear His love for Jerry and the promise in the Gospel. I asked for the privilege of telling him a story. He said yes, and I told him that while I was at college I taught gymnastics to a group of children whose parents were on the faculty of the college. Just a few years after I graduated, I learned that one of those students, who was now 15 (I think), had developed terminal cancer. One day when his father visited him at the hospital he said to his father, 'I know I'm saved, but would you go through the plan of salvation one more time? I want to be certain I am right with Jesus.' I then said to Jerry, 'I believe you have heard about this salvation before, but I am wondering if you would want to go over that again just like that young boy.' He said yes, and I had the wonderful privilege of seeing God change Jerry's heart and hear him ask for forgiveness and for Jesus to be his Lord. To top this, his family asked me to tell this story at his funeral so a lot of people heard the Gospel story.

We are reminded by the chaplain that God does not given up on people and that sometimes the hardest and most difficult cases melt under His grace. One last story illustrates this point:

> [He was] a lawyer who would not accept visits from a chaplain. He had been disbarred because of getting involved in the wrong side of some political activity. He had lost most of his life in the bottom of whiskey bottles. Then came the day his significant other and caregiver convinced him to accept the chaplain. Praying with a sense of desperation all the way to his home, I arrived to pray another prayer as I walked up his sidewalk. It went something like this, 'God, if you don't help me, we are all in deep weeds.' (real heavy theology, right?) Well, I am convinced that almost every word that came out of my mouth was inspired, and while this patient was non-verbal, he had tears on his cheeks and nodded his head yes when asked if he wanted to ask Jesus to forgive him and become his Lord. He also agreed to my

praying with and for him. Here again, much of that story was shared in a larger group setting.

Although the chaplain's ended on a note of encounters with these cases that are discussed were positive and victory, in reality, Chaplain Simpson writes,

> Most people die as they live; that is, if they have not wanted to have anything to do with God or Jesus in their life, they most likely will not want to change that when they are dying. Death-bed conversions, in my opinion, are more myth than reality. That idea has affected my life inside and outside my 'professional' life. It has impacted my life in my church and increased my desire to develop relationships with non-believers who may give me the opportunity to share the faith.
> In the Hospice chaplaincy, I have been moved (forced) outside of the safe walls and relationships I had within my church life. Until I became a chaplain my life had been inside the church or relationships created by the church. I talked and taught about being involved with the 'lost' but Hospice has given me the opportunity and forced me to respond. Perhaps the most precious lesson I have learned is that I am absolutely dependent on God for wisdom, for courage, for understanding; I am totally dependent on His grace. You are called to a home, to a hospital, or hospice, to help a hurting, upset family; you realize you do not know them or their needs and then you must rely on God who does know and trust Him to use you for His glory and good.... Hospice for me has become a mission field to patients, to their families and sometimes to Hospice employees. Thank you, Lord, for using me.

Chaplain James Demaray, Hospice of the Bluegrass

ALTHOUGH A RELATIVELY NEW CHAPLAIN to Hospice, James Demaray has evidenced a special compassion for the dying. The hospice chaplain, says James, "helps people experience life in the midst of death – helps people process life in view of eternity." He goes on to say that sometimes the dying have visions and sometimes think they are going crazy. The role of the chaplain is to be Christ's presence to them without necessarily speaking in

Christian (church) terms. The chaplain must listen to their stories and be sensitive to what is going on in their mind, body, and soul. Some, according to Demaray, have spiritual experiences that may not always be recognizable as centered in God or Christ. The chaplain starts where they are and leads them, if they are willing, into the presence of God and eternity.

James recounts the story of a hospice family that demonstrates how Christ can work in a barren land if He is given the time, the room, and the opportunity. This family had already had a history of being under hospice care before Chaplain Demaray took their case:

> All three of their male children had the same disease and it was fatal....They had no spiritual background on which they could build. The oldest child was in the hospital dying. The young boy was agitated....While asleep, his uncle, who died of the same disease, visited him and told him that everything would be all right. A great peace came over the young boy and the next morning he told the mother about the dream/vision and the peace it had brought to him. The experience opened the family to the idea that there was something beyond the reality in which they lived. After this, it was easy to discuss spiritual matters with them. When I began my ministry to them they had a picture of Jesus on the wall and pictures of Mary, Joseph, and the baby Jesus on the refrigerator. They were now open to prayer and God's goodness....

This powerful story of how God brought hope to a hopeless family demonstrates again the importance of recognizing the call of clergy into the Hospice chaplaincy.

CHAPTER EIGHT
CORRECTIONAL FACILITY CHAPLAINCY

IN 1980, THERE WERE 400,000 state and federal prisoners in America. By 1994 the number had climbed to one million. In 2001, that number had soared to two million. Today there are nearly 2.3 million prisoners. While America has about 6% of the world's population, we have 25% of its prisoners. This unprecedented number of incarcerations has left our prisons nearly 20% over capacity, according to James Logan's book <u>Good Punishment? Christian Moral Practice and U.S. Imprisonment</u>: "...this mass incarceration as a social policy aimed at controlling crime has significantly transformed families and community dynamics and exacerbated racial division."(pgs. 65-66). Logan found in his study that to process and house the 2.3 million prisoners costs the United States $50 billion a year.

Since a majority of inmates come from poorer communities and are minorities, the greatest hardship falls upon those already struggling to make it in life. In addition, many prisoners have little education, often suffer from some form of early childhood abuse, and have experienced some drug or alcohol abuse. Emotional problems are also common and most inmates, if not all, are in desperate need of some kind of deep healing.

The inmates are almost certain to be faced with violence, the threat of rape, and a code of silence. You rat and you die! Power is the game. Stripped of privileges, activities, friends and family, men and women are stretched to the breaking point. In Matthew, Chapter 25, Jesus urged the Church to visit those in prison. At this writing, our denomination has endorsed a total of approximately fifteen chaplains to correctional settings - local, state, and federal. Many other Free Methodist pastors work as volunteer chaplains at county and city jails as well as detention centers.

Requirements for correctional chaplains are similar to those of the military. Federal and State requirements are also similar, while local jail and detention-center requirements may vary. Although the Correctional Chaplain is required to meet certain educational, ecclesiastical, physical, and age requirements, they are also urged to have additional training in such areas as suicide prevention, CPE, victimology, substance abuse, conflict management, PTSD/CISM, and the Criminal Justice System.

The correctional chaplain offers ministry to the prisoners, the staff and the families of both. The chaplain is to the prisoner the presence of God in the midst of barbed wire, steel doors, armed guards, loneliness and suffering. The prisoner often feels defeated, angry, depressed, hopeless and alone. Into this dark and depressing world the chaplain carries the light of God, preaching, as Isaiah did, "…the good news of release to the captive…." Unlike the patient in the hospital, the prisoner may spend many years of his or her life behind bars. The prisoner's situation is different in that he/she will suffer failure and despair apart from family, friends and other normal support systems. Naomi Paget and Janet McCormack, in their book The Work of a Chaplain, capture this estrangement:

> The judge said,' Three strikes and you are out.' Now he was in jail awaiting trial. His mother was allowed to visit once a week but for six days and 23 hours he was alone. His friends had abandoned him, his family was ashamed of him, his church had lost contact with him, and his employer had given up on him. He had no one. The isolation and estrangement was like an open wound--painful and likely to bleed him to death. The chaplain's daily visits were like balm on open sores. (pg. 64)

A few months ago, an old friend of the writer, who now serves in the leadership of Gideon's International, came through Wilmore, Kentucky. He had recently attended a regional meeting of the Gideons in New England and had heard a Baptist pastor from Tennessee tell an amazing story of his incarceration in the Quantico, Virginia, Marine Corps Detention Center in the late '70s. As a young sailor he had become a drug abuser, which landed him in a jail cell. He told the Gideons that while awaiting a courts martial, which would result in his being awarded a Bad Conduct Discharge, a chaplain visited him, and had given him a Gideon New Testament. He began to read it and was wonderfully saved. To my surprise, he said that I was the Chaplain. We have since been in communication and I now know the rest of his story.

After being discharged from the service, he answered the call to preach and is now a successful pastor and Christian speaker.

Chaplain Elijah Owen, Corcoran Prison

CORRECTIONAL CHAPLAINS HAVE THE TOUGHEST ministry in the world, but because the need is so great, so is the satisfaction and fruit. The Free Methodist Church has been blessed to have great men and women answer the call to correctional work. Because of his long tenure and excellent work under the most difficult circumstances, Elijah Owen has earned the title of "Dean" of our correctional chaplains. I first met him while traveling as the Church's Endorsing Agent in the '90s. Elijah was from the Southern California Conference, and was serving as senior chaplain of the California Maximum Security Prison at Corcoran. Here, the toughest and worst criminals in the state are incarcerated. Chaplain Owens began as a social worker who had connections with prisons. He was invited by the prison to apply for a chaplain position and was eventually hired as chaplain at Susanville Prison. Later he was appointed to the position at Corcoran which is one of the most notorious prisons in the country and has the distinction of being the first maximum security prison built specifically for that purpose from the ground up.

This facility has been featured in a number of television documentaries, including 60 Minutes. Corcoran was designed to house 5,000 male inmates but has now expanded to contain 10,000 or more. Among their infamous guests are Juan Corona who murdered 25 people; Charles Manson who orchestrated the Sharon Tate murders; Sirhan Sirhan who killed Senator Robert Kennedy; and Mikhael Markhasev who killed Ennis Cosby, son of Bill Cosby. The prison has a history of gang violence within its walls which has resulted in a number of deaths. Some charged that the staff staged gladiator fights between prisoners and shot prisoners needlessly. A major investigation was launched, but only a few isolated incidents were found to have occurred. This was the atmosphere in which Free Methodist Chaplain Elijah Owen ministered as Senior Chaplain.

In his role of providing pastoral care to inmates, Elijah had to rely on the recruitment, training and supervising of a large number of volunteers. His responsibilities seemed overwhelming to me, yet he seemed to accept this stressful challenge as simply a part of his sacred calling and proved himself as a valued member of the prison staff. When I recently asked him what he would say to a young man or woman who was considering prison chaplaincy, he replied he would urge them to do so because it was a satisfying place to do ministry and preach the Gospel. He also spoke highly of the strong support he received from the prison administration in the performance of his religious duties.

Prison chaplains walk a delicate line every day between their role as a staff member of the prison and their role as a caregiver and advocate for the incarcerated. Because of his position and closeness to the prisoners, the chaplain is not without risk every day he/she goes to work.

Chaplain Myron Henry, Oregon State Corrections

It was 1982 when Navy Chaplain Myron Henry stood on the deck of the Battleship USS MISSOURI, BB63 at the Puget Sound Naval Base, in Bremerton, Washington, to be retired in a traditional Naval ceremony. When Myron and Ruby walked off the ship, it was not to go home and rust out. Instead, Myron was taking a chaplain position with Oregon State Corrections. Myron states of his new job:

> I was glad I had military experience before going to prison. The adjustment of working within the walls at a maximum security prison was easier because of the similarities. Moving from an autocratic/authoritarian system to one of rigid standards of discipline and security was not that difficult. However, being able to put trust in my clerks and other members of the chapel presented a new problem. It was verboten to let any inmate have the keys to cabinets, office doors, etc. The chaplain was required to get the mail, sign for all office supplies, and to accompany the clerk who carried these back to the office. The reason being there was always the chance that the inmate, along the way, might make a drive on the box of supplies or try to blackmail the clerk in some way.

Chaplain Henry confessed that it took him some time to understand the criminal mind. He suggests that anyone beginning a jail or prison ministry should consider what they confront in the inmates. The chaplain is dealing with people who have issues with anger, depression, anxiety, attitude towards authority, family separations, lack of self discipline, lack of control, a tendency to violence, lack of trust, just to name a few. Because these folks are unable to deal constructively with these problems, they end up in prison, often have their prison sentence extended or, when they are released, return repeatedly.

During religious services and religious group meetings, their lack of discipline is clearly evident. Most regularly come late, often attend sporadically, and will interrupt meetings by getting up to take a smoke or talk with a friend. Most cannot sit for long periods. They are restless, often as a result of drug burnout.

On the other hand, Chaplain Henry writes, "It is awe-inspiring to see people in prison change. To hear their testimonies is thrilling." In terms of presenting the Gospel of Christ to inmates, he states, "Christ is best presented in a personal relationship with the inmate." In most cases, the chaplain did not find religious literature all that helpful.

Chaplain Henry states that the revolving door – that is, recidivism (prisoners returning again and again after release) – is seen as a major problem, Like other correctional chaplains, he sought to engage local churches and groups to help the prisoners find their way back into the community and into a supportive church. Our own Free Methodist church near the prison, Salem Free Methodist, came alongside Chaplain Henry to help provide emotional and spiritual support for discharged inmates. For this he was very grateful.

Two interesting experiences are related by Chaplain Henry's wife, Ruby, since he, at this writing, is in failing health. The first incident concerned his relationship with a Muslim prisoner:

> One day an inmate passed the chaplain in the hallway and asked him to put his name on the list for a sack lunch for the Ramadan Fast. The proper way was for the inmate to submit an official request in writing. Before returning to the office, Myron forgot the verbal request. The man did not get his Ramadan sack lunch. The inmate then sued Myron because he said he missed 1,000 blessings.

A second story dealt with a request for a marriage ceremony:

> A woman prisoner was notorious for having shot her three children. Her story was made into the TV movie "Small Sacrifices". During her prison stay in Oregon she became engaged to a man in the penitentiary. She requested that Chaplain Henry contact Jimmy Swaggart, the famous TV evangelist, and invite him to come to the prison to perform the ceremony. To her unhappiness, Myron denied her request. She remains in prison.

At his prison retirement ceremony, the service began with a drumming ceremony provided by the American Indian inmates. This consisted of four drum songs, one of which was created especially for Chaplain Henry's honor. After the other chaplains gave their speeches, Myron and Ruby were invited to the front of the chapel by the inmates. A small choir then sang, "Thank you for giving to the Lord," followed by inmates walking up the aisle one by one to either shake Myron's hand or give him a hug. According to Ruby, "It was truly a moving experience."

One of Chaplain Henry's finest accomplishments was to use his influence to urge the State of Oregon to hire their first woman chaplain. That woman turned out to be our own Free Methodist Imo Smith, who had just retired from the Army.

Chaplain Dennis Demond, Ft. Leavenworth Military Prison

THE DISCIPLINARY BARRACKS AT FORT Leavenworth, Kansas is the only military prison left in America after the Navy closed its prison in Maine in the 1960s. This writer visited the Naval Prison when it was operational and was so impressed with the ministry opportunities that he requested duty there repeatedly but was never assigned. However, one of our finest Army chaplains, CH (LT COL) Dennis Demond, did a tour as chaplain at the military prison at Leavenworth, Kansas. Here, military enlisted who have been convicted by military courts martials, as well as Department of Defense personnel sentenced to at least five years, are imprisoned, along with military officers. This would include those who were convicted of spying or passing classified information to our enemies.

The military prison should not be confused with the Federal Leavenworth Prison located nearby. Military prisoners actually assisted in building not only the Military Prison but the Federal Prison as well. The Disciplinary Barracks sit on about twelve acres overlooking the Missouri River and have a cemetery where inmates who die in prison and are not claimed by members of their families, are buried. About 300 grave sites are there including fourteen grave sites of German prisoners of war who were executed in 1945 for murdering fellow prisoners. The prison also has a death row on which eight prisoners await death by lethal injection at this writing. Chaplain Demond was assigned to corrections although he was not trained to be a correctional chaplain. However, he served with distinction and at his retirement was awarded the Legion of Merit, one of our country's highest awards, for his excellent service.

During Chaplain Demond's assignment, the prison provided Christian, Jewish, Muslim and Native American worship services for its 1400 inmates. He supervised three military chaplains with support staff and about 100 volunteers. His primary ministry was to maximum security and protective custody inmates, and to inmates with death sentences. The boundaries are clearly outlined regarding the ministry these special inmates may receive so as to guard the chaplain-inmate relationship and protect the inmate and institution. The inmates are accorded religious rights and access to the chaplain but their freedom is limited because of their crimes.

The Barracks contracted a Native American to lead the Native American services; however, this leader did not always come when scheduled. Since this service was conducted next door to the chaplain's office, the chaplain monitored what went on in the space. A problem arose when the worshippers burned sweet grass with a mixture of sage, cedar, and juniper. The small fire produced a lot of smoke, filling the adjacent areas and the chaplain's office. For security reasons, after the ceremonies, sniffing dogs were brought in to make sure that grass was only the good kind. It was. The problem continued, however, when the smoke increased in spite of the chaplain's appeal to decrease the fire.

Finally, the authorities were called to test the air during the service. It was found to be so contaminated that the medical department called the chaplain, his staff, and all guards in the area to the clinic for further testing. The chaplain and his staff tested positive for several chemicals. From that time on, when the Native Americans met for worship the chaplain personally rationed the amount of grass to be burned. The worshippers were not happy with the chaplain but no one got sick. Worship continued, and peace was restored to all.

Since prison breaks are always a concern, I asked Chaplain Demond if they experienced any breaks while he was at Leavenworth. He said, "Yes, one." Three inmates working in the kitchen hid in a garbage dumpster and made it out the gate on the back of a garbage truck. Their luck ran out, however, when a motorist on the road observed the prisoners peeking their heads out of the dumpster and alerted the prison. If you have ever smelled the gas emanating from a full dumpster of decaying garbage, you can understand why they were looking for fresh air.

Chaplain Debra Reitz, Muncy Maximum Security Prison

KEYSTONE CONFERENCE IN PENNSYLVANIA is proud of their correctional chaplain, Debra Reitz. Debra serves at the Muncy Maximum Security Prison. This famous women's prison began as the Industrial School for Wayward Girls, for those sixteen to thirty years of age. Now it houses about 1,300 women, part of a female prison population of 75,000 in American correctional facilities today. The prison has a death row with three presently awaiting execution. The prison population refers to them affectionately as the "Three Amigos." In an article in Sunday Times, (August 31, 2008) entitled "The Pink Mile: Women On Death Row", writer Ariel Leve was given great liberty in visiting the prison and interviewing staff and inmates, including those who had murdered their husband's girlfriend, their own husbands, and some even their own children.

Leve does an excellent job of pointing out the differences between male and female inmates. She notes that women are less violent, do not join gangs, generally do not seek power over one another, do not keep secrets, do not hold malice, often have been abused, tend to internalize their emotions, and have more depression than men. One of the injustices the older inmates feel keenly, is that crimes they committed in years gone by often resulted in a life sentence, but today, the same crimes may get a person no more than five years.

It is into this environment that Chaplain Reitz goes each day to represent Christ's presence.

Chaplain Imo Smith, Washington State Department of Corrections

SHE DREAMED OF BEING A missionary. She became a first-grade elementary teacher, then a church pastor, then an Army chaplain. After nine years in the Army and serving the troops at bases in Texas, New Jersey, Washington State, Korea, and Saudi Arabia (during the Gulf War), Imo Smith left active duty and was accepted as a prison chaplain in the Oregon Department of Corrections, joining Myron Henry, a retired Free Methodist Navy chaplain. After a number of successful years in Oregon State Corrections, Imo has now moved to the Washington State Department of Corrections where she serves as the Department Chaplain for her facility. Here she provides for and manages the religious programs for a large number of offenders. Imo not only provides for basic Protestant worship and Christian Education, but also supervises a host of contract clergy and volunteers who provide religious coverage for other faith groups. Her duties also include counseling inmates, acting as an advocate for families and offenders, providing classes on anger management, communication skills etc. As a corrections chaplain, Chaplain Smith has one of the most demanding ministry assignments of all our chaplains.

The State provides concise documents that guide the chaplain's daily ministry and they are the most definitive this writer has seen, surpassing even that of the military. For example, in the Department of Corrections Policy Directive, Document 560-200, entitled "Religious Program" is stated the religious rights of the incarcerated. It says,

> The Department recognizes the inherent and constitutionally protected rights retained by the incarcerated offenders to believe, express and exercise the religion of their choice. The Department extends to individuals under their supervision

those opportunities necessary to practice religious freedom that is consistent with the security, safety, health, and orderly operations of the facility.

This is one of the strongest statements on religious rights you will find anywhere. The same document spells out the general content of the institutions' religious programs. "Religious programs will foster positive values and moral practices that develop healthy relationships, especially with families." At the same time the Department is clear to say they do not recognize or endorse any particular religious faith. It states that the chaplain will be supervised by the Department Superintendent and is charged with managing the entire religious program, although the chaplain is not expected to conduct all services for all religious groups. The Department has a strong statement on "proselytizing" that is of special interest:

> The chaplain, contract chaplains, other staff members of the community, and offenders, may not solicit unsolicited, unwanted or forced attempts to persuade another individual to convert from one religious belief to another, or criticize religious beliefs of others, within the grounds of any Department facility. Nothing in this provision will prohibit the sharing of information regarding an individual's religious belief.

Another important part of the document guiding the chaplain's ministry deals with the chaplain's management of other religious groups who have the same constitutional right to worship as do those of the chaplain's own faith. In order to provide proper space, equipment, supplies, and other requirements to support particular faith groups, twenty faith groups are identified along with all the resources needed to sustain their practices. This means that the corrections chaplain must be fully knowledgeable of a large number of faith groups so that he or she can assist them in exercising their religious rights. It is the responsibility of the facility chaplain to see that the spiritual needs of all offenders are met appropriately. This is a formidable task. Our correctional chaplains must be exceptional people by any measurement. In a job void of glamour and church accolades, they faithfully go about their ministries daily, behind iron bars, and out of sight. Most of what they do is for the eyes of God alone.

Chaplain Smith comes alongside a grieving mother, an inmate who is losing custody of her beloved child. The chaplain listens to her pain, sympathizes with her, prays for and comforts her, and promises to be there to support her in the future. There is no fanfare here, no clapping by a congregation. It's only Jesus working in a dark and lonely place to give hope. Commenting on her ministry, Chaplain Smith writes:

> I have been a chaplain in men and women's facilities covering minimum, medium, close custody and intensive management units to include segregation. In addition I have covered in patients medical clinics with suicide watch dry cells where no article of clothing or items like a mattress or cot were allowed until the offender reached a level of trust. I am responsible for the programming of all religious rites that are mandatory to an offender being able to practice their religious preference. (It should be noted that this is a right that is extended to offenders that is not even enjoyed by all free people.) It takes a lot of team work with other staff and volunteers including training regarding procedures, religious property, and diversity of religious practices.

In addition to leading her own Christian ministry and managing volunteers, Chaplain Smith must also conduct religious services for other faith groups, keep the peace, answer all complaints, and comply with all Department policies regarding religious practice. In addition, she must interface with clergy and families who have family members incarcerated in the facility, and cover her actions and decisions with clear and timely paper work that would stand up to the toughest scrutiny or a court of law. What if every pastor had to do this? I would guess it would diminish the number of ministerial candidates in seminary and reduce ordinations to a slow dribble.

Chaplain Smith walks us through just a part of an ordinary day's schedule:

> Today I have already opened building C where the chapel is located, discussed Islam personal property with an offender, supervised three offender chapel clerks, talked with a family about an emergency notification request that had been denied by staff, responded to phone calls, e-mails and distribution material, supervised the viewing of a religious video, read a chapter in the book <u>100 Women of The Bible</u>, supervised the cleaning of assigned spaces, met with a DOC staff touring the facility, worked on scheduling Christmas and Revival services for 2009 and 2010, prepared and submitted a fund request for markers to design choir smocks, and it is not yet 1 p.m.

But lest we think that the corrections chaplain's ministry is all detail, Imo also shares her joy in seeing her flock come to Christ, grow in the faith and look forward to returning to their families to face the future with the Lord. She is especially encouraged by the spiritual growth she sees among those with whom she shares spiritual leadership. She invites offenders who would probably never have had the opportunity to participate in religious leadership in a local church to risk serving the Lord and others. To their surprise they love it.

Chaplain Chris Mogenson, Broome County Jail

HE WAS A MEMBER OF the high-profile Maranatha Church of the Nazarene in Milford, New Jersey. His pastor was an ex-addict. Chris describes his formative years in the church as developing in him a "street-oriented Christian experience." When he transferred to Eastern Nazarene College (ENC) as a Religion major, he joined the prison ministry team. By his second semester he was elected chair of the team.

In 1983, he graduated from ENC with a BA in Religion and enrolled in the Nazarene Seminary in Kansas City, Missouri. Here he worked with Catholic charities and specifically with men serving life sentences in prison. In addition, he began working at the Kansas City Rescue Mission. When Chris tried to connect the Rescue Mission residents with local churches he found resistance from members and leadership. He writes:

> During my tenure at the Rescue Mission I started to see some of the ugly side of the local church. An attempt to bring the Rescue Mission residents to local church services was met with passive-aggressive resistance from both parishioners and clergy alike, which left me angry and suspicious. I have remained amazed at how those who call themselves Christians could so blatantly ignore the Gospel, especially Matthew 25, and yet focus on a myriad of outward signs of holiness.

Through these experiences and others, such as pastoring a poverty-stricken bilingual church on the border of Mexico, as well as a predominantly African-American Caribbean church in New Jersey, God continued to form Chris's heart for a non-traditional ministry. After a CPE course and a short year pastoring in a coal-mining county in Pennsylvania, he made the decision to pursue a position in corrections.

In 2000 he moved his family to upstate New York and took a position as Director of Jail Ministry for the Broome County Council of Churches as well as the position of Coordinator of Chaplains for the County Sheriff's Office. He also assumed the duties as Chaplain for the Community Crisis Chaplain Corps through the Council of Churches. All the work and spiritual formation Christ had been doing in Chris, now came to full blossom. He had found his niche.

Today, up to 4,000 inmates transition annually through his correctional facility. He says of the correction system at large,

> The Christian Church needs...to realize that this system is terribly flawed and does not work. It is not an answer and we have a responsibility to keep huge portions of our population from being seriously disenfranchised. Over two-thirds of these people will return in a few years. In the field, we often call this "serving a life sentence on the installment plan." Many of these people have serious mental illnesses and developmental disabilities. Still more are caught in cycles of addiction which exacerbates other issues of poverty, racism, illness and inequity. One of the most overlooked aspects of the correctional chaplaincy is the corrections officers. The chaplain serves both sides of "the thin blue line". Many of the correctional officers as well as officers who patrol the highways are serving sentences in another form. The raw ugliness of the world is so often in full view day after day and the cumulative affect can be devastating to them and their families. Ministry to these people is immensely important.

The Broome County Correctional Facility has a county mandate to maintain religious programming for all inmates. In keeping with this goal, Chaplain Mogenson conducts no less than five worship services a week. He also facilitates worship for the Roman Catholics and the Muslims by providing for a priest and an Imam to conduct services for their own.

Over 100 volunteers are recruited, trained, and coordinated by the chaplain to assist him in an active and broad ministry throughout the facility. They provide programs for family literacy to sharpen inmates' literacy skills and also help them read and record stories for their children at home. The chaplain's office is on the frontline for pastoral care, intervention, death notices, and crisis management with the families. They also work with the inmates' reentry program by outfitting them with clothing, hygiene kits, connecting them to churches and, when needed, providing a one-way ticket home.

Perhaps the most important ministry, however, is offering the inmates and their families a listening ear. After the chaplains listen, they offer to pray with the inmates, share scripture with them, and invite them into a personal or deeper relationship with God who wants to be their ultimate help. Last year, Chaplain Mogenson completed his eighth year of teaching a spiritual formation class, using a curriculum which he had written. His curriculum has been adopted and adapted as a model in other correctional facilities.

So, does jail ministry make a clear difference in peoples' lives? Here are some testimonies from Broome County Jail. One inmate, who accepted Christ during a jail worship service, described his life before conversion as miserable and worthless. He said he had lived with addictions, crime, anger, and severe illness but now, with a sparkle in his eye, he speaks of how his life has improved since he became a believer.

Others have told the chaplain that they didn't mind serving their sentences in jail because it was there they found a good place to worship, and worship was enjoyable and helpful to them. One inmate simply wrote "…Thank you. You are blessed for your dedication and compassion to us inmates…." Another penned, "…I would like to thank you for reaching out to my family.…I would also like to know if you could give me a Bible to read because I have never read the Bible in my life…."

Yet another wrote,

> During the most desperate time in my life of being jailed, I was confused, lost, lonely, and feeling unloved. I am thankful to have had a service of ministry. The one on one ministry has guided me in changing my life, it was the starting point for me to hear that God loves and forgives, giving me the desire to learn more about God and how I can change the way I live. When a stranger, a minister, takes time to help you understand that you as a person are worthy deserve a chance to make changes in your life, it is more than just words. I have a sense of hope and a feeling of self worth only because there was a jail minister, someone who cared enough to listen to me and help me understand God and how God can help me.

Finally, one inmate writes,

> The music allows me to show emotion that every-day jail life can darken. It is rejoiceful. Jail ministry has changed who I once was and the way I think, feel, and act. I am truly

grateful that there is a ministry in this jail and, I hope, in all jails, because it can be a starting point for so many people's lives as it has been in mine. It has helped me change my character to care about others and want to help and support others, to share the good news with others, and help direct them to God....

The wonderful work represented by Chaplain Mogenson's ministry in the Broome County Jail is typical of the kind of ministry our Free Methodist correctional chaplains are offering all across this country. They carry a heavy load and are often at risk. The challenge they face is overwhelming. They and their families are worthy of our prayers. We are proud of their service

Chaplain Harry Timm, Twin River Correctional Center

FOLLOWING HIS RETIREMENT FROM THE Army chaplaincy, Chaplain Harry Timm took a position as senior chaplain at the Twin River Correctional Center in Monroe, Washington. The Center housed male sex offenders. One of Chaplain Timm's ministries was to invite people outside the prison to visit inmates and to help them transition back into society. After six years Chaplain Timm retired because of ill health and went to Heaven. As a tribute to his work, his widow, Maribelle, continued to participate in the visitation program which she saw as having great value. She still speaks of the satisfaction she had in befriending an inmate, visiting him over an extended period of time before his release and successful reentry into society.

Volunteer Pastors

TRIBUTE IS ALSO DUE TO the countless pastors who have voluntarily provided pastoral ministry to county jails, detention centers, and prisons across America. These closed communities are not always easily accessible to the pastors who take time out of their busy schedules and sometimes travel some distance to visit the incarcerated.

Chaplaincy: Being God's Presence in Closed Communities

Chaplain Debra Reitz

Chaplain Chris Mogenson

Chaplain Tom and Barbara Holman

Chaplain Sam Shreffler

Chaplain Paul Lattimer

Chaplain Wesley Dodge

CHAPTER NINE
RETIREMENT COMMUNITY CHAPLAINCY

The Aging of America

AMERICA IS IN THE PROCESS of a dramatic transformation and it is not about politics or global warming. While much of our culture has been focused on youth and young adults, many have failed to recognize the marching throng of new seniors headed our way. In the 1990s social scientists warned that dramatic changes were coming due to the aging of America. Now, nearly twenty years later these changes are here and the church, politics, the media, health care, marketing, recreation and education are beginning to feel the impact of this revolution.

Following WWII there was a baby boom of 75 million births in America between the years of 1946 and 1964. These baby boomers are now coming into their senior years, and, as James Knapp points out in his book, The Graying Of The Flock , we haven't reached the peak yet. (p.14) Today, there are more senior citizens than teenagers. In 1900, seniors in America made up only 4% of the American population (Catch the Age Wave, Win and Charles Arn, p.28). By the 1990s they represented about 13% and they are projected to reach 20% or more in the next twenty years. (Knapp, p.14) The reasons for this are many. The baby boom is only one factor. The growth of technology, health care improvements, availability of care, better diet, additional monetary resources, additional travel, recreation, social interaction and continuing education are but a few factors affecting the increase in the number of seniors.

E. Dean Cook

New Seniors

WRITERS OFTEN REFER TO TODAY'S seniors as "new seniors". They are given this title to differentiate them from their predecessors of fifty to sixty-five years ago. So, how do today's seniors differ from those of the past? "New seniors" are more prone to volunteer, seek positions of leadership, engage in continuing education, keep themselves informed, practice generosity, and travel. They are more open to new ideas, spiritual growth, and participation in church and community. In short, they are looking to live a rich and productive life, not simply to spend their years on the shelf and die.

In addition to the local church's ministry to their own seniors, senior retirement facilities have sprung up across America with their own religious programs. Most of these centers have a volunteer part-time or full-time chaplain. Our Free Methodist Church is associated with several outstanding retirement communities: Heritage Ministries, headquartered in Jamestown, New York, oversees multiple retirement centers; Warm Beach Senior Community is located near Stanwood, Washington, north of Seattle, and Woodstock Christian Life Services is located in Woodstock, Illinois, north of Chicago, to name only three.. These senior communities provide both independent and assisted living. Warm Beach and Heritage also provide skilled nursing care as do other facilities near Woodstock. These are all faith based and non-profit organizations. Heritage and Woodstock both trace their founding back to 1886, while Warm Beach had its beginning around 1967.

These communities provide a wide variety of activities in the arts, music, continuing education, travel, physical fitness, swimming, etc., as well as a variety of opportunities for spiritual growth, fellowship and worship. All three retirement communities employ chaplains to provide quality pastoral care to residents.

It should be pointed out that there are a variety of alternative living arrangements for seniors today. They may participate in shared housing, senior apartments, adult foster care, nursing homes, family care homes, special care units, rehabilitation facilities, dementia care, day care services and CCC, which stands for Continued Care Communities. In the Continued Care Communities, one may enter at the independent living stage, later advance to the assisted living stage, and finally reach full care before death. The qualifications required of a chaplain to serve such a community are of the highest order.

In our study we will examine the chaplaincy ministry at the senior communities of Woodstock, Heritage Ministries, Warm Beach, Park Pointe, and Townhouse. At this writing, Chaplain Randy Waller provides ministry to Woodstock; Chaplain Sam Shreffler assisted by Chaplain Gerald Haglund and Chaplain Ray McGinnis, serve the Heritage Ministries; Chaplain Wesley Dodge serves Warm Beach; Chaplain Paul Lattimer serves Park Pointe; and Chaplain Doug Vogel serves Townhouse.

Heritage Ministries Chaplaincy

The Heritage work began as a vision of Reverend Walter Sellew of the Genessee Conference. The following is a description of his vision.

> In the vision it seemed that he was in a crowded street where thousands of children were rushing to quick destruction. His heart being deeply touched, he made every effort to stop them but to no avail. At last, in desperation, he threw himself on the street with arms outstretched from curb to curb, thinking they would respect his body. But no, on they rushed faster and faster over his body and through his fingers. At last he awakened with his heart broken and himself weeping bitterly.("Our Goodly Heritage: A History of the Gerry Homes" by Mr. Charles T. Lake and Rev. Harold S. Schwab, 1986, p. 5)

This vision motivated Pastor Sellew (later Bishop) to start plans for an orphanage in 1886. In that same year the work was incorporated as The Orphanage and Home of The Free Methodist Church. In 1894, thirty-five children and ten aged persons were at the home. In 1897, a note was made in the Home records that, "There has [sic] been no deaths or sicknesses and our expense for medicine and medical attendance for the year has been only $2.50." The incorporation document was amended in 1959 to read, "… to establish, operate and maintain a home for aged persons; to establish, operate and maintain a home for destitute and abandoned, neglected and dependent children; that all directors shall be members of the Free Methodist Church…."(Ibid, p.4)

In 1901 a new fully-furnished building, was completed for the aged at a cost of $14,000.. By 1903 they could not accommodate all the applications for residents. Four years later the General Conference of the Free Methodist Church officially recognized both Gerry Homes, as it was now called, and Woodstock Homes in Illinois.

One of the special blessings was that natural gas was discovered on the Gerry Homes property and a well was sunk. For the next sixteen years the facility used this well for the need of all the main buildings, resulting in a great utilities savings. Meanwhile, the Homes farm provided much-needed milk, meat and produce.

Orphanage Closed

In 1965 the orphanage closed due to increasing state requirements, and financial restraints. However, it left behind a wonderful record of caring for over 1,800 children that did not slip through Bishop Sellew's fingers. Now Gerry Homes focused on becoming a total retirement and extended care facility. The facility changed its name again, this time to The Heritage Group and later to Heritage Ministries. This change was fitting because of the expanding ministry. Gerry Homes would not only acquire other facilities in the area but would develop a whole new retirement community in South Carolina known as Rock Hill. They would later sell this development but Free Methodist residents would continue to live there. A Free Methodist chaplain employed by Heritage would continue to serve under the new ownership.

Chaplain Ministry at Gerry Homes

Gerry Homes was founded as a ministry, and pastors played a major role in providing spiritual care for its residents. From 1910 to 1968 the pastors appointed to the Free Methodist Church in Gerry, New York, were also appointed to Gerry Homes. These pastor/chaplains read as follows from the Genesee Annual Conference Year Book appointments:

> N. B. Martin, C.E. Pike, J. O'Regan, A. Baldwin, C. L. Silverton, G. B. Tingue, J.H. Harmon, A.E. Hydahl, C. D. Bates, F. M. Hendricks, C. J. Edwards, S. O. Smout, E. Butterworth, H. L. Dibble, R. M. Cooley, T. B. Simpson, Walker Jordan, Ray L. McGinnis, Evan Hessler.

Later, part-time chaplains included Hershell Hutt, Thomas Simpson and Herbert Olver. Full-time chaplains included Raymond McGinnis, 1993 to 1999; Virgil Dey, 1995 to 2004; Gerald Haglund (Heritage's first non Free Methodist chaplain), and Samuel Shreffler 2000 to the present.

Ray McGinnis played a key role in developing the chaplaincy at Gerry and served as chaplain twice. His strong ties with the Conference, his reputation as a compassionate pastor, his leadership as a delegate to General Conference and trustee of Roberts Wesleyan College, drew added attention, helping to recruit volunteers to serve at Gerry Homes. For many years and for much of the denomination, Ray McGinnis was the face and heart of Gerry Homes. He always spoke enthusiastically about Gerry Homes wherever he went. Chaplain Sam Shreffler, who followed McGinnis, is an equally capable and energetic chaplain. Shreffler is now the President of the Free Methodist Chaplains Association.

For the last ten years Sam has provided oversight for the Heritage Ministries. During his tenure, he has placed a strong emphasis on bringing people to Christ and inspiring the residents to do the same. He states that he has personally led an average of twenty people to the Lord each year he has served the community. The following are examples of just a few lives that he has touched:

> We had a mother and son who lived here as residents. The mother was a part of our assisted living and her son had his residence in the nursing home. Neither of them had a relationship with God. The mother was first to give her heart to the Lord. It was a simple and solid decision she made to serve God, following many open discussions about a God who desired a loving relationship with her. Following her decision, we worked together to reach God's love to Andy (her son). His breakthrough to Christ came when his mother died. Andy wanted to see his mother again in Heaven and opened his heart to know this Jesus his mother had found.
>
> This man who came to us had been the mayor of Jamestown, was involved in the Rotary, traveled extensively with his wife, but finally his health broke, his wife passed away, and he came to us suffering from despondency. Over the first four to six months he was with us, I was able to build a relationship of God's love to him and though he never had time for church when he was younger, he began to come to our services. He soon became hungry to have a relationship with God and invited Jesus to enter his heart and life. There is still despondency from time to time but he has learned to trust Jesus to help him walk through the hard times.
>
> I ride a motorcycle and one of the staff members asked if I did weddings. "Yes," was my simple reply, "but I would need to meet with you over time." I did and was invited to be a part of their special day if I would bring my motorcycle along. The woman staff member, in the process, gave her heart to Jesus as she prepared for her marriage. We are still praying for her husband.

One of the characteristics of a good leader is one who sees their life reproduced in the lives of others. Chaplain Shreffler's love for souls has been reproduced in the lives of his flock. They, too, are urged to share Christ with their neighbors. Many of them do so. One lady on the campus asked the chaplain for some Bibles. When he asked her how many, she replied, "Five." It turned out that she had led five of the staff to Jesus and wanted to give them each the gift of a Bible.

Heritage Ministries continues as a star model for ministries to retirement communities.

Warm Beach Senior Community

WARM BEACH SENIOR COMMUNITY GREW out of a large development of land located on the Puget Sound near Stanwood, Washington. The property was purchased by the Pacific Northwest Conference of the Free Methodist Church in the late 1950s. Dr. Charles Kirkpatrick, one of the two District Superintendents of the Conference was the visionary for the camp/conference grounds. This writer's wife, Ruth, worked for the Conference Office during the early development of the facility. Her maternal grandfather and grandmother, moved from Kansas to live on the undeveloped property as a carpenter and caretaker. The site work on the property began around 1959, with the retirement community following in about 1967. Today Warm Beach is one of the finest conference grounds, camps, and retirement communities in the whole Pacific Northwest. One of the early retirement community directors was Chaplain Harry Ansted.

One of the early chaplains was Rev. Maurice Miller, former Superintendent of the Oregon Conference. In 1999, Pastor Wes Dodge, also from the Oregon Conference, was urged by his father-in-law, Rev. Lyle Northrup, a Warm Beach resident, to apply for the chaplain position. Though a bit reluctant at first, Pastor Dodge finally applied and was accepted. He is a positive and compassionate spirit and has been very successful in this assignment. At this writing, he and his wife, Joyce, have been ministering at Warm Beach for a decade.

Chaplain Dodge models his ministry at the community after a parish ministry. He provides worship, preaching, Bible studies and daily devotions, as well as visiting regularly among the residents. According to his own testimony, he considers his ministry of presence as one of the most important elements in his pastoral care, quoting the words of the Baptist pastor Aaron-Ott:

> While our Bible exposition and ministry acumen is helpful, it must not crowd out this ministry of presence that is

more clearly shown in Jesus' ministry than any other of his practices....We will find all our exegetical and expositional skills painfully under-utilized in chaplaincy. Very little of that will come out in the chaplain's greatest moments of effectiveness; those being when people simply need a chaplain to be with them, cry with them, eat with them, drink with them, laugh with them....

In this spirit, Chaplain Dodge relates a charming story of which he was privileged to be a part:

Don Hamm and Virginia Phillips met in a rehabilitation room of the nursing department in the Warm Beach Senior Community. Both were in their eighties. Both had lost spouses in previous years. Both had suffered similar strokes, affecting the opposite sides of their bodies. Both were confined to wheel chairs, and both were lonely.

Don and Virginia became acquainted while taking rehabilitation together. They began to carry on frequent conversations and to spend more and more time together. They found themselves uncommonly attracted to each other. They decided to get married. Thus, it was one beautiful day in 2004 in the Beech Wood lounge that a crowd gathered, music played, and Don and Virginia made their way down the aisle in wheel chairs, stopping before the chaplain. Since their strokes affected opposite sides of their bodies, they could firmly hold hands.

There, in the presence of witnesses, they went through the time-honored ritual of marriage. 'I, Don, take you, Virginia, to be my wife.' 'I, Virginia, take you, Don, to be my husband.' After the pronouncement, sealed with a kiss, Don and Virginia wheeled out of the chapel and began new scenes of life together.

The nursing staff had arranged a two-person room into a nice apartment with two beds pushed together in the middle. For over two years Don and Virginia lived as husband and wife, to the great enjoyment of observing family and friends. Don told the chaplain several months after their wedding: 'Chaplain, God has given me the most wonderful woman!' After Virginia's death her family related that the last two years of her life were made wonderfully happy by her marriage to Don. From depressed, discouraged people, both became beautiful examples of God's amazing grace. However, Virginia was often reminded that by arrying Don she became a Virginia Hamm.

Park Pointe Village

IN JUNE OF 2000, THE Heritage Group purchased sixty acres of choice land in South Carolina to establish a new retirement village called Rock Hill. Numerous Free Methodists were drawn to this beautiful area located only twenty miles from Charlotte, North Carolina. The Free Methodist Area Bishop, Bishop Richard Snyder, took a special interest in this development and began the construction of his own retirement home nearby. Also, a Free Methodist church was established near by and a pastor was appointed. It was the vision of the Heritage Group Area Bishop that this development would become a key part of a larger plan to expand the Free Methodist Church in the South. However, due to financial concerns, the development was sold in 2005 to another Christian Group who renamed the retirement center, Park Pointe Village.

The Chaplain of the Village, Rev. Paul Lattimer, a Free Methodist, has continued to serve for the past nine years. Lattimer is greatly respected and loved by his Park Pointe flock in great measure for his courage, rich experience, and kind spirit which he brings to the community. Paul graduated from Asbury Seminary in 1971, but, after pastoring only four years, suffered a debilitating stroke. The stroke left him with limited speech, hearing, and comprehensive skills. Many would have given up their pastoral dreams at this point, but not Chaplain Lattimer. For the next four years, he says," I underwent an extensive rehabilitation program…where I got a degree in endurance, patience, and human adaptation."

Two years later, Pastor Mendel Daningburg invited Paul to become his Associate Pastor at the Ransomville, New York, Free Methodist Church. For the next six years Paul served the church where Pastor Daningburg and the congregation became an important part of his healing process. In 1985 he was appointed Senior Pastor of the Binghamton FM church where he served successfully for the next fifteen years. During this assignment Paul not only proved he could fulfill all his pastoral duties, but also excelled by growing his flock numerically and spiritually. Then, in 2000, Pastor Lattimer was asked to take the chaplain position at Rock Hill Retirement Village. Few chaplains ever came to a retirement-center position with more qualifications. Chaplain Lattimer is truly a miracle of God and one of our finest chaplains. When he says to a suffering member of his flock, "I understand," they know he really does.

The mission of Park Pointe Village is found in these words:

> Park Pointe Village is an ACTS Retirement-Life Community. ACTS is committed to providing security and peace of mind to all residents by being the pre-imminent provider of retirement life services, meeting residents' social, personal, health and spiritual needs in a Christian atmosphere, graced with loving-kindness, dignity, sensitivity, honesty, and respect without prejudice to any individual or preference to any particular faith or creed.

Lattimer leads a Spiritual Life Team (SLM) that consists of nine members from the community. This team assists the chaplain in ministry and directs the disbursement of offerings and charitable gifts. In 2008 the Board received over $25,000 in offerings and gifts, and gave $23,000 to global missions. The spiritual life ministries of Park Pointe not only serve within their community but reach out to the community and the world beyond.

The chaplain's office provides a wide variety of spiritual growth opportunities for residents. Those opportunities include Bible studies, prayer groups, grief groups, devotionals, and worship services for Protestants, Roman Catholics, and Episcopalians. In addition to the more mobile residents, Chaplain Lattimer has a vital ministry to those who, as II Corinthians 4:16-17 states, are "...wasting away outwardly." He writes of a ninety-year-old man, who is wasting away with cancer, yet faithfully attends his Bible discussion group in order to grow in his faith. He also shares the story of a woman suffering from dementia. She could not hold a normal conversation yet she could sing the old hymns of her faith. The Chaplain also speaks fondly of a man and his spouse who suffer from Alzheimer's, yet come to worship where they experience comfort in God's presence. Lattimer is an example of how the Free Methodist Church is continuing its rich tradition by ministering to all people in diverse places, circumstances, and ways.

The Townhouse Retirement Community

LOCATED ON THE NORTHEAST CORNER of Fort Wayne, Indiana, is the Townhouse Retirement Community. This not-for-profit facility provides residents not only a safe and comfortable place to live but also the cultural, medical, and shopping opportunities of a major city. The development began in 1965, and is now a full independent-living retirement village along with assisted living and nursing care.

Chaplain Doug Vogel is appointed by the Free Methodist Church as chaplain to Townhouse. His ministry is unique in that his setting is not associated with the Free Methodist Church directly and his position as a chaplain is a unique model. After serving Free Methodist parishes for twenty years, Doug began to look for new opportunities. When he heard of a part-time chaplain position at Townhouse, he applied and was accepted. During the next year he served as part-time chaplain while taking courses for a degree in education. At the end of the first year, the social services director retired. At that time the manager of Townhouse invited Vogel to come on the staff full-time with half-time devoted to the chaplain's position and half-time devoted to social services. After considering how the two positions blended together, Vogel accepted the position of chaplain/social services associate.

Vogel feels quite at home serving in these two roles, finding that they overlap at a number of points, complimenting each other. He leads worship, conducts prayer meetings, intervenes to help solve relational problems, interacts with outside health-care representatives, and provides counseling. He also arranges for legal support needed by residents, such as Powers of Attorney and Notary Public, among others. Townhouse and Chaplain Vogel may have created a whole new model for chaplaincy, especially in this day of shrinking budgets. Although Chaplain Vogel is still relatively new in this position, it is clear from his testimony that this ministry is highly successful and has brought great satisfaction, along with new energy to his life and to the community.

Air Force Village West

AIR FORCE VILLAGE WEST NEAR Riverside, California, deserves honorary mention in this chapter because two of our retired Free Methodist chaplains – Harry Ansted and Myron Henry – make their residence here. In addition to both Ansted and Henry having served here as volunteer chaplains, both men and their wives have been active in the religious program of the community. This is one of several quality military retirement communities across America that employ full or part-time chaplains.

Summary

IN SUMMARY, THESE SNAPSHOTS FROM a variety of retirement ministries remind us why it is vitally important for our church to provide and endorse chaplains to these settings. Our Free Methodist chaplains are particularly effective in ministering to this growing segment of our society. As our culture ages, we can expect retirement communities to grow and most will demand the care of a chaplain.

CHAPTER TEN
CIVIL AIR PATROL CHAPLAINCY

A SPECIAL THANKS TO CAP Wing Chaplain, Lieutenant Colonel Robert Magee, Jr., who served as a contributor and consultant for this chapter. We will tell Bob's story later. Soon after WW II began, Gill Rob Wilson, head of the New Jersey Division of Aeronautics, presented the idea for a Civil Air Patrol organization to Mayor Fiorello La Guardia of New York City. Already we were concerned with our long coastline and the potential for the enemy to sabotage our utilities, threaten our airports, sink our ships, and do damage to our ports. Wilson found a ready host of volunteers following the attack on Pearl Harbor. An amazing 40,000 civilian pilots and interested airmen signed up to assist in this voluntary civil defense and rescue effort. Some offered their own small aircraft, others purchased planes, still others overhauled old and outdated planes and pressed them into service.

Congress Establishes CAP

IN 1941, CONGRESS OFFICIALLY RECOGNIZED the CAP as a vital volunteer organization that served a special need for the country. Thus, Congress gave it the same official standing and recognition as that of the Red Cross. It was made an auxiliary of the Army Air Corps and would receive limited support from our Army air bases. The CAP adopted as their insignia a white triangle on a blue field to show their connection to the nation's civil defense program. A red propeller was later added to the white triangle. The rank system of the Army Air Corps and its style of uniform was also adopted.

Small CAP operational centers sprang up all along our nation's coastlines. Single-engine aircraft were authorized to fly up to fifty miles out to sea to look for enemy submarines and to assist in the rescue of seamen from sinking ships, of which there was a growing number. Multi-engine planes were authorized to fly up to 200 miles out to sea. Others flew utility lines, watched power plants and other strategic targets the enemy might be interested in taking out. But a major part of their mission was humanitarian, with search and rescue dominating. During WWII these small planes and their crews provided an amazing volunteer service to our country.

CAP Mission

DURING THIS PERIOD, ACCORDING TO the CAP Museum, CAP pilots flew more than 24 million miles over water. They spotted and reported sighting 173 enemy submarines, attacked fifty-seven, damaged seventeen and sank one. Although the CAP was noncombatant, after they observed a German submarine run aground on a sand bar off the Florida coast and were helpless to damage it, the Army Air Corps agreed to let a limited number of aircraft carry a small bomb which might have injured a German submariner had it fallen on his head! Their primary role remained in spotting, reporting and assisting in rescue. During the war effort, fifty-nine CAP pilots were killed, with twenty-six lost at sea. These volunteer airmen became affectionately known as "Flying Minute Men."

According to Chaplain Magee, the CAP performs 90% of all air and ground search and rescue and has over 60,000 volunteers. Their present Commander is Major General Amy Courter. CAP welcomed women pilots from its inception but they were restricted from flying missions that were considered combatant. Most recently CAP played a major role in the emergencies surrounding 9/11 and Hurricane Katrina.

An important arm of the CAP is their Cadet Program which is comprised of young men and women between the ages of twelve and eighteen years of age. This program trains and provides practical experience in airmanship and aerospace for youth. A full one-tenth of every Air Force Academy class consists of former CAP cadets, according to Magee. The CAP organization remains an auxiliary of the Air Force and can be integrated into the Air Force during times of national emergency.

In 1950, the CAP formally established their own chaplaincy, the only all-volunteer unpaid chaplaincy in the world. Today there are approximately 1,200 CAP chaplains serving all across America. Its educational and professional standards are the same as for military chaplains with one major exception: there is no age requirement. The eight national regions of the CAP offer an annual Chaplains Staff College to train CAP chaplains. Courses taught include Pastoral Crisis Intervention, Terrorism and Disaster Response, and other courses related to CAP work. These college courses are required for promotion in rank and are conducted on Air Force bases with Air Force support.

Chaplain Mervin Russell

THE EARLIEST RECORD WE HAVE of the Free Methodist Church's involvement in CAP chaplaincy comes to us from Mervin Russell, who served as our denomination's Director of Youth and the Servicemen's Department in the late 1950s. In 1996, Russell wrote about his experience in the CAP in a publication called "Living Water." The article was entitled, "My Angel Flew Alone":

> I had never been in the military, so to get a better feel for the Service, I joined the Civil Air Patrol and was appointed Wing Chaplain for the State of Indiana with the rank of Lt. Colonel. My duties were to enlist chaplains for Indiana, train them and make visits to them. One day I was flown in an Air Force transport plane to five different Indiana cities to visit five different chaplains. On several occasions I flew with cadets to Air Force bases for their training. Once I flew the Free Methodist Youth Department's Bonanza to Whiteman Air Force Base in Georgia [actually in Missouri] to serve as CAP Chaplain for a CAP conference. The base was a Strategic Air Command Base at the time with high security so I landed at the local civilian airport and called the base on the airplane's radio and asked permission to land for the conference. I was astounded to receive permission to land so I fired up my engine, flew across town and landed at the base. When I taxied to the parking place, I was met with a car load of military police with drawn weapons to challenge me. When I explained that I had received permission from the tower to land, they did not believe me and called the Officer in Charge. The Officer confirmed my story and the head of the security party replied, 'I have been here many months and you are the first civilian plane I have ever seen land here.'

In a 1961 issue of the Light and Life Magazine, Chaplain Russell appears in a photo wearing his CAP uniform. The photo accompanied an article he wrote as Director of the Servicemen's Department. Russell was a strong recruiter for CAP chaplains and was, according to records, our first CAP chaplain.

Chaplain Delbert McLaughlin

BISHOP MARSTON, IN A LETTER to the Servicemen's Director dated 1954, addresses a near-tragedy that befell one of our CAP Chaplains in California. The chaplain, Delbert McLaughlin, was flying from Riverside to Sacramento with fourteen other CAP chaplains to attend a chaplains training conference. They were flying as passengers in an older Air Force plane with a crew of four when one of the engines caught fire. The pilot was unsuccessful in putting out the fire until it threatened the loss of the wing. At this point the pilot ordered all aboard to bail out. Fortunately, there were enough parachutes aboard and the passengers quickly donned them. All jumped, including the pilot and crew. As all eighteen floated down from the sky, the plane was observed to crash in a ball of fire. Due to the good graces of God and the pilot, all landed safely, without loss of life. However, Chaplain Mc Laughlin became entangled in his chute lines and received serious leg injuries. No records are available to tell us of his recovery period or his later involvement in CAP.

Chaplain David Paul Smith

ALSO IN ANOTHER 1961 "LIGHT and Life" issue, a photo appears of David Paul Smith, a popular pastor at Turlock, California, in his CAP chaplain's uniform. The article states that Chaplain Smith was Wing Chaplain of the Yosemite CAP Group. He wears the wings of a pilot upon his chest and extols the CAP Chaplaincy as a ministry that brings satisfaction and opportunity. The article reads like a thinly-veiled attempt to recruit interested Free Methodist pastors into the program.

Chaplain Robert Magee

WHILE PASTORING AT FORESTVILLE, MARYLAND, Robert Magee met fellow-Free Methodist pastor George Wood who was a CAP chaplain. Wood shared his experience with Magee and urged him to join the organization. He applied, was accepted and for the next twenty-eight years he served as a CAP chaplain, rising to the rank of Lieutenant Colonel. Magee holds the distinction of being our longest-serving and highest-ranking CAP chaplain. Upon request, he provided this account for our history:

> My first assignment was as squadron chaplain, duties included teaching a class on Moral Leadership to cadets,

conducting religious services on weekends, and providing counseling. In 1986 I was asked to serve as Wing Chaplain of the National Capital Wing. The Wing covered squadrons in Maryland, Virginia, and the District of Columbia and included the oversight of 12 CAP Chaplains. While Wing Chaplain, I became a member of the Military Chaplains Association and was the first CAP chaplain to be awarded the Distinguished Service Award by that organization. In 1999 I was promoted to Region Chaplain for the Middle East Region. This Region covered six states and seventy chaplains. In this capacity I was a member of the National CAP Chaplains Board, serving with the other seven Regional Chaplains. My primary responsibility was the planning of the annual Chaplain Staff College, an accredited professional development required course for CAP Chaplains.

In 2003, Chaplain Magee retired from the pastorate and resigned his position as CAP Region Chaplain. He and his wife, Carolyn, moved to Florida where they enjoy their retirement. However, after only a year into retirement, Bob volunteered as CAP Chaplain at the South Brevard Cadet Squadron in Melbourne. In this capacity, he is again ministering to some of our nation's finest youth who may some day serve as astronauts..

During his long career, Bob has been honored as a Chaplain of the Year, and has received the Distinguished Service Award, the Commander's Commendation Award, and the Exceptional Service Award for his Region. Chaplain Magee has represented the Free Methodist Church and his Lord with distinction, humility, and integrity to those who love to fly.

Recently, at a Fourth of July concert conducted on the campus of Transylvania University in Lexington, Kentucky, the local CAP cadets opened the evening's celebration by presenting the colors. They were an impressive group and seeing them reminded the writer once again of the great work our CAP chaplains have done on behalf of the Free Methodist Church.

E. Dean Cook

Chaplain Robert and Carolyn Magee

Chaplain Mervin Russell

Chaplain David Paul Smith

Chaplaincy: Being God's Presence in Closed Communities

Chaplain John and Belva Owen

Chaplain John Leffler

Chaplain Burton and
Jauneta Kincaid

Chaplain David Nicholson

Chaplain Joy Ireland (right) and counsellee

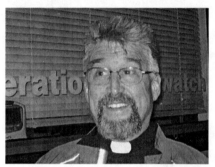

Chaplain Richard Reynolds

Endorsing Agents and Bishop
L-R: Dean Cook, Robert Crandall, Bishop Thomas, Robert Barnard, Rex Carpenter and Harry Ansted Jr.

CHAPTER ELEVEN
POLICE AND FIREFIGHTER CHAPLAINCY

Chaplain Burton Kincaid

WE OWE CHAPLAIN KINCAID OF East Michigan Conference and the Michigan State Police, special thanks for being a major contributor for this particular chapter. In the early 1990s I visited Pastor Kincaid at his home in Michigan soon after he had moved to a new conference assignment. He told me that when his moving van arrived at the new parsonage, he was surprised to find his house surrounded by state patrol cruisers. To the amazement of the neighbors, the patrol officers were not there to arrest anyone but rather to help the Kincaids move into their new home. It was the officers' way of saying "thank you" to their chaplain. Their presence was a testament of their acceptance of him as one of their own, that they valued his ministry to the Michigan State Highway Patrol.

Over the years, Kincaid says, the police and firefighters have moved from a reactive relationship with chaplains - which he characterized as, "Don't call us, we will call you"- to a proactive relationship that now says, "Please spend time with us and let's work together." Upon appointment as a State Police Chaplain in Michigan, each chaplain is presented a certificate that reads:

> Know all men by these presents that said chaplain is appointed a member of the Chaplain Corps...for the avowed purpose of helping officers maintain a respect for human dignity based upon the Brotherhood of man and the Fatherhood of God. To help build a firm moral foundation and provide spiritual incentive and admonition that will

> strengthen the self esteem of all officers, and to be available to department personnel at times of tragedy and emergency within the limit of his time, place and ability. (MSP)

Prior to 1970, there were only a few police and firemen chaplains across the country. In the late 1970s, this writer, while assigned to the Quantico Marine Corps Base, was also assigned duties as chaplain to the FBI Academy. In my association with the FBI and other law enforcement officers from around the world whom they trained, I was astounded to discover that most agents and officers had no chaplain support available in their workplace. These public servants and their families faced the day to day dangers, stresses, and separations without the support of spiritual ministry from someone inside their community. The same was true of firefighters.

When he lived in Flint in the 1970s, Kincaid recalls two police officers getting into a disagreement over who was going to drive the patrol car. The argument escalated and they exchanged gun fire in an attempt to settle the dispute. The police department and the city responded by creating their first police and firefighter chaplain position. Our own Free Methodist Burton Kincaid was a charter member of that chaplaincy. Sometime later, two Flint firemen drowned in a rescue operation. The police chaplain was called to minister to city firefighters and their families. Out of this tragedy was born the Flint Fire and Police Chaplaincy.

Since the 1970s, the number of police and fire departments that have assigned chaplains has steadily grown. Free Methodist police and fire chaplains, along with others, played vital roles in the aftermath of the 9/11 bombings in New York City and Washington D.C.. They listened, consoled, wept with and prayed for police, firefighters, and their families who had lost relatives and friends. These chaplains could move easily among the grieving people because they had already established a relationship with them. Religious differences mattered little. Compassion and understanding were central.

John Wambaugh, in his book, Echoes of The Darkness (1987), states that the public has seldom understood the real danger inherent in police work. (His statement is equally true of firefighters.) He goes on to says that such duty has never been particularly hazardous to the body, but it has always been a threat to the spirit (p.292). The argument for spiritual ministry begins here. It is Wambaugh's strong contention that these public servants, police and firefighters, must be seen as real people with real emotional and real spiritual needs. Popular newsman Paul Harvey, in an article published in 1981, stated:

> A policeman is a composite of all men, a mingling of saint and sinner, dust and deity…the most needed and the most unwanted…he must be able to start breathing and stop bleeding…he must know everything and not tell…know where all the sin is yet not partake.…he must be able to whip two men twice his size and half his age without damaging his uniform or being brutal.

Police and firefighters, by the very nature of their work, tend to be extremely private people. tThey are a close-knit group that cares deeply about how they are perceived by the public and by their fellow workers. To be seen as weak can be damaging to a career where competition and competence are rewarded. Therefore, they are not prone to risk being seen visiting a counselor or clergyperson for personal problems. However, a chaplain who stops by to have a cup of coffee, hang out with them or ride along on patrols, becomes accepted as one of them. Once the chaplain is invited "inside" and becomes a trusted friend, these public servants will begin to open up to the chaplain because now the chaplain has gained credibility in their community. Acceptance is never a given. The chaplain must earn the right to be an insider by walking, talking, working, and riding with them.

During his chaplain duties, Kincaid has been involved in domestic disputes, shootings, raids on drug houses, gambling houses, and houses of prostitution. He has ministered to people at drownings, at auto accidents, and other crises. But it has also been his privilege to minister in happier circumstances, such as weddings, baptisms and promotions. The chaplain represents God's presence to a community that struggles with keeping a healthy balance between work and home, between high stress and peace of mind and soul.

Two high honors have come to Chaplain Kincaid with his ministry in law enforcement. First, he was invited by the FBI Academy at Quantico, Virginia, on two occasions to lecture law-enforcement officers regarding the chaplaincy and their personal need for spiritual resilience. Secondly, he was honored by being elected as President of Michigan State Police chaplains It is also very important to note that most police and firefighter chaplains are volunteers. They serve because they feel called by Christ to their vocation.

Chaplain John Owen

JOHN OWEN IS ONE OF the Church's pioneer police chaplains. His large frame and big heart have left a legacy of police and crisis ministry work across many states and cities. John traces his urge to be a police chaplain back to his seminary days when he visited Chicago as a part of an inner city ministry. During this experience, John was assigned to ride along with a police officer. Immediately, he saw the opportunities to minister to police officers and people in crises. When he moved to Minneapolis, John's church was only a few blocks from the police precinct. One evening he took some tea and cake down to the station to share with the officers. Because of the suspicious nature of the officers they refused to eat the cake until John took the first bite. Once he indulged, they eagerly ate also, and a friendship began that eventually led to John becoming their chaplain.

Later, a police officer who was a strong supporter of volunteer police chaplains was elected Mayor of the city. With his encouragement, other pastors now joined John and formed a corps of chaplains that took turns one day a month riding with and serving the city's police. In 1973, John met with seven other police chaplains in Washington, D.C. and formed The International Conference of Police Chaplains. This professional chaplain's organization now has over 3,500 members and certifies chaplains to provide counseling and support to police officers and other emergency services.

Chaplain Owen went on to establish police chaplaincies in Seattle, Buffalo, and Washington D.C. It was while in Washington that John was charged with a crime and placed in jail. While in a parking garage, his attention was directed toward a car whose alarm had gone off. He went over to the young lady standing by the car and asked if he could be of assistance. John showed her his police chaplain identification so as not to alarm her. Totally misreading his motives, the woman apparently thought he was impersonating a police officer and was harassing her because of her race. Chaplain Own was arrested as a result of the woman's complaint and jailed on charges of impersonating a police officer. He was ordered to appear in court. Needless to say, a crisis prayer call went out, and a lawyer was consulted. Like Daniel in the lions' den, John was finally delivered and the police joined in the celebration of his release. He was fully exonerated.

The Washington D.C. Crisis Chaplain Corps, led by John Owen, was housed in the United Methodist Building in the "Heart of The Hill" from 1997 to 2003. The Methodists generously provided office space for John at no cost to him. Here he headed a significant ministry in our nation's capital during one of our country's most critical times. The city was very much on edge following the terrorist attack on 9/11.

Not long after 9/11, an anthrax attack was made on the Brentwood Post Office facility in Washington, D.C. which resulted in deaths. This was the post office where the Crisis Chaplaincy had its mail box. The facility was immediately shut down and quarantined. All mail at this post office was confiscated by Security. This national security crisis now visited a crisis upon

Chaplaincy: Being God's Presence in Closed Communities

the Crisis Chaplaincy Office because the ministry was totally dependent on financial support sent in by contributors through the Brentwood Post Office. The Maryland-Virginia Conference of the Free Methodist Church and the Bishop's Famine Relief Fund responded by assisting the ministry until the post office matter could be resolved. At the time, the Crisis Chaplaincy was the only Free Methodist ministry inside the Capital beltway.

At this writing, John and his wife, Belva, have resigned their pastoral appointment in central New York to - you guessed it – begin another full-time ministry in crisis chaplaincy. The work, which comes under the New York Conference, is called The Crisis Chaplain Corps, and is located in Elmira.

Firefighters

NO DOUBT OUR FREE METHODIST firefighter chaplains know of the fine work of The Fellowship of Christian Firefighters, International, headquartered in Fort Collins, Colorado. This organization, made up of active-duty and retired firefighters, publishes the magazine, "The Encourager", and has as their guiding Scripture, Hebrews10:25, *"Let us encourage one another... all the more as you see the day approaching."*

The purpose of the organization is as follows:

To glorify God in the fire service.
To find fellowship together for individual growth in the Christian life.
To serve the cause of Christ through the church of one's own choice.
To encourage those in the fire service in their Christian life.
To share locally in planned fellowship meetings, individual contact, and prayer.
To share nationally through participation in fire conferences and expositions.
To bring all Christians in the fire service to a common goal of praying for the fire service and it's members.
To share on an international basis through an Annual International Conference.
To have contact internationally with fellow firefighters Christian.
To care for widows; meeting spiritual as well as physical needs.
To care for firefighters in times of need.
To place Bibles in fire stations.
To distribute New Testaments to individuals in the fire service / EMS.

Their Vision is: *"That I may know him and the power of His resurrection,"* (Phil. 3:10) Their Mission is: "To take the vision to the fire service community by evangelism, empowerment, and encouragement."

E. Dean Cook

Chaplain Dan Clegg

FREE METHODIST LAYMAN DAN CLEGG serves as FCFI International Director, and Regional Director for Indiana, Ohio, and Kentucky. This retired firefighter writes of his last night's duty on the Indianapolis Fire Department after thirty-two years. His experience reminds us of the importance of having spiritually-minded firefighters and chaplains to these closed communities. This incident also reminds us that firemen do more than fight fires – they are also involved in rescue:

> January 2, 2001, the last night of my thirty-two-year and eight-month career as a firefighter for the Indianapolis Fire Department arrived. My emotions were mixed; joy for the future, unbelief that so many years had passed. As a youth I had hoped that if an emergency would happen it would be on my shift. Tonight, I just wanted a peaceful entrance into retirement. Instead, it proved to be a sleepless night with two of the most unique runs of my career.
>
> The clock struck 1 a.m. I am prepared to get some rest when the tones rang. We were dispatched to Washington Street near Station 18 for an O.B. run. We rushed to the door and were greeted by a young man.
>
> 'Where's the expectant mother?'....'She's not here. She gave birth a few minutes ago, cleaned up, got into the car with a neighbor and drove off with her baby.'
>
> 'Why'd she do that?' I asked incredulously.
>
> 'She's a crackhead.' he replied.... we called the police department to continue the search. I had an uneasy feeling about the destiny of the infant and hoped the mother had not discarded the baby in a trash dumpster. After searching the dumpsters and coming up empty, we called the police department to continue the search.
>
> As we entered the fire station, the alarm went off: another O.B. run, approximately 4 ½ miles from the previous one. Climbing into the driver's seat, I jokingly said, 'It's probably our mother and baby from our prior run on Washington Street....We rushed into the house and found a young lady and baby sitting contentedly.
>
> 'Where's the expectant mother?' I asked. 'How far along is she?'
>
> 'I'm the mom and this is my baby. I delivered her myself. She was full term.' I looked at the baby lying in

her arms in a bright blue sleeper, taking in the world around her. I smiled.

'The delivery was no problem,' she said. 'I had prenatal care.' As she continued to speak I realized she was the missing mom from the previous call. I inquired of her health. 'I haven't touched any crack since I got pregnant,' she proudly announced.

Moving into medical mode, I inquired about the afterbirth and learned it was still attached. I gloved up, clamped the cord, examined the baby and informed the medic in route that the baby had been delivered an hour earlier.

Back at the station sleep evaded me. I kept thinking about that little baby delivered at home by her own mom. I had jumped to conclusions that could have altered the care I gave this new family. I pray not! As I remembered the motherly glow on the mom's face I thought about another birth 2,000 years ago to a woman whose character was also questioned. Humbly, I asked God to continue to help me not to judge. Then I prayed that this birth would change the young mom's outlook on life permanently and lead her to Him.

Chaplain John Lefler

A FEW YEARS AGO, A devastating tornado cut a wide swath of destruction across southeastern Indiana. When it was all over, several communities were left in ruins and the casualties were high. Rescue teams, fire departments, and law enforcement all joined hands to deal with the aftermath. Free Methodist Chaplain John Lefler found himself at the center of this emergency response; first, because he pastored a church in the area; but more importantly, because he was chaplain to the Evansville Fire Department and had built a strong relationship with them.

When duty called, John was already trained and ready to go. During this major disaster he ministered to families in their shock, grief, and loss. He also ministered to the response teams that worked long and tireless hours in search and rescue. When a major crisis like this occurs, pastors do not have time to seek training – they must respond immediately. Relationships built carefully over time become vitally important.

Chaplain Lefler, while pastoring both in Michigan and later in Indiana, had always volunteered as a police and firefighter chaplain. He also took the time and effort to qualify as a certified fireman himself. Upon moving to Indiana, John contacted the Evansville Fire Department Chief and volunteered to be their chaplain. After listening to his proposal, the Chief invited him to join the team. This began a long-term friendship which enabled John to lead the Chief back to the Kingdom and into his church as an active member.

In addition to acting as chaplain to Evansville Fire Department, Lefler is also chaplain to the Indiana State Police. He has served as an officer in the Fellowship of Fire Chaplains, and as a member of the International Conference of Police Chaplains and the Federation of Fire Chaplains. The following incident relates an unusual way God used Lefler's ministry to these closed communities:

> As a part of my ministry, I send weekly prayer notes that I'm especially praying for them that particular week. On one ordinary Monday, I mailed my prayer notes. On Wednesday of that week, I received a phone call from one of the troops, saying that he had received my note and was very upset about it. He wanted to know if the command had told me things about him and wanted to know why I had sent that note to him. I explained that I sent several a week in alphabetical order, and it was his turn to receive one. He was so angry that he asked me to never send him another one. On Friday of that same week, I received a phone call from another troop to tell me that the first troop had been involved in a shooting and had been wounded and hospitalized. I immediately went to the hospital, knowing that he had not been accepting of my prayer letter. The hospital took me immediately into the emergency room. The troop was on the table, his wife beside him, and two other troops standing nearby. When he saw me enter the room, he said in a rather loud voice, 'Hey, everyone, meet the man that saved my life.' He then told everyone how I had been praying for him that week and that he was sure it was the only reason he survived the criminal's attack. He never again objected to my praying for him and told many others how God used me to save his life.

Kincaid, Owen, Clegg and Lefler are typical of a number of fine Free Methodists who are serving as police and firefighter chaplains. Others include Chaplain David Nicholson with the Noblesville, Indiana, Police Department; Chaplain Mearl Bradley with the Michigan State Police, and

Chaplain Norman Channel with the Iowa State Patrol and Mt. Pleasant Sheriff's Department. Our Church owes a great debt to these fine pastors and laypersons who give their time to shepherd law enforcement and firefighter personnel and their families. Well done!

CHAPTER TWELVE
CAMPUS CHAPLAINCY

MANY OF OUR EARLY AMERICAN colleges and universities were led by presidents who were ordained clergy. These presidents also acted as spiritual leaders of the campus. However, in 1808, an event happened that would signal a change in religious activity on American campuses. It happened in the small, all-male Williams College, located in Williamstown, Massachusetts. Here, some students under a burden to take the Gospel to the world, held a prayer meeting at a haystack near the campus. During this meeting, they felt led to organize The Brethren Association, with the goal of taking the Gospel across the world to those who had never heard. This" Haystack Prayer Meeting" went down in American church history as the beginning of our nation's world missions program. Thanks in part to this early campus effort, America sent out her first overseas Christian missionaries, Adoniram Judson and Luther Rice. The William College religious movement was student and lay led. In addition to inspiring America's first world missions program, this small campus group also inspired similar religious organizations and associations on other college campuses. The Church quickly recognized the need to support this good work and give guidance to these spiritual yearnings.

Several denominations and faith groups offered their support by helping fund the movement and by sending the first chaplains to campuses. Many of these early chaplains were not an official part of the schools administration, faculty or staff. Instead, they were recognized as representatives of their sponsoring churches sent to support students. The schools welcomed them so long as their activity met a need and supported the welfare and quality of life of the students. Since the chaplains were usually employed and funded by their own faith group, the chaplains and their religious activities center were normally located off-campus but within easy walking distance, for the convience of the students. Some universities, such as Stanford in California, and Transylvania in Kentucky, built on-campus chapels for ecumenical religious use.

In cases where the college or university employed the chaplain, the institution determined the description of the chaplain's duties, in addition to providing an office and meeting space. The difference between institutionally funded chaplains and those funded by their faith groups, was that in the first case, the chaplain was required to minister to a pluralistic student body, while chaplains in the second case could choose to minister only to students of their faith group. This also meant that the campus chaplain, as part of the institution, was required to meet a high standard of education, training, and experience. Today, campus chaplains are usually required to be accredited by the Association of College Chaplains, (the agency that seeks to set the professional standards for campus chaplains), hold a Masters of Divinity degree and be ordained by a recognized religious body.

Specific duties of the campus chaplain vary from school to school. In the case of faith-based colleges and universities, the chaplain may be designated as the Dean of the Chapel. In that capacity, he/she will select the chapel speakers and, along with student leaders, plan religious programs and activities to meet campus needs. The chaplain may also organize, plan and send students on short-term mission trips, at home and abroad.

Roberts Wesleyan College

In the past, the Dean of Students often doubled as the college chaplain. This had its draw backs however, since the Dean was also the one who enforced student discipline. In 1990, when this writer took a position in the Religion Department at Roberts Wesleyan College in New York, the campus religious program was led by the Dean of Students. Upon observing this structure and its inherent weakness, I approached the Provost and the President about making a change. They responded by asking me to survey twenty-five colleges of similar size to see what was being done on their campuses. The study was completed and recommendations were prepared. As a result, in addition to my teaching duties, I was also asked to take on the responsibilities of a newly-created position: College Chaplain. In this capacity, I would serve one-third time under the Dean of Students.

Although the position was not structured as I would have liked, I accepted the challenge knowing that most new positions require a transitional period in order to discover what works, and what does not. Using student leaders to help plan and lead the spiritual-life programs gave students ownership. As a result, the spiritual interests of the students grew rapidly, until they were initiating their own Sunday evening worship services, led entirely by them. They also initiated an outreach program to the campuses of the Rochester Institute of Technology, the University of Rochester, and other schools in the area. Students from these campuses joined the Roberts students in their worship services on Sunday evening. In addition, the chaplain and students opened a prayer chapel on campus, developing it into a special place for solitude, prayer, and counseling. What happened over the next two years was a pleasant surprise. The spiritual life of the campus was genuinely renewed.

Doug Cullum, who was just completing his doctorate, was appointed campus chaplain upon my departure and continued to build upon these spiritual gains. Upon Chaplain Cullum's appointment to the faculty of the newly-established Northeastern Seminary on campus, Pastor Tom Kilburn, Youth Pastor at Pearce Memorial Church (the college church) was appointed as Chaplain. Tom was an excellent choice since he knew the students well and had worked with many of them as a staff member of the church. Jonathan Bratt is now the acting chaplain at Roberts Wesleyan College. He shares with us the role he is now assigned. The following are five areas of ministry that make up Jonathan's role as Campus Chaplain.

Director of the Chapel:

The Chaplain plans chapel services and speaks in chapel on relevant issues pertaining to the lives of the students and their spiritual development. Speakers from on and off the campus are utilized. Chapel services are the most public and most attended of the spiritual life opportunities. (Attendance is taken; students are allowed a limited number of absences).

Director or Coordinator of Student Ministries:

Students sincerely want to live out the call of God in their lives. Chaplain Bratt tells of a student-initiated, student-led prayer vigil lasting 48 hours, for the purpose of praying for the entire campus. Students also participate in worship teams, inner-city ministries, compassion ministries, as well as youth and children's ministries. Because the students rotate in and out of college constantly, there needs to be someone with "big picture" focus on coordinating ministries and keeping the contacts. The chaplain is that person.

Pastoral Care:

Jonathan writes:

> The chaplain is always ready to counsel, mentor, give spiritual direction, or pray with a student in need. Discerning when

the 'teaching and ministry moments' come is a great skill that must be learned, because these moments are usually not planned or scheduled; they come in the midst of walking across campus, eating a lunch, planning a service, or attending a meeting.

Mission Trip Coordinator:

This is not always the direct responsibility of the chaplain, but the chaplain is very much involved in helping the students gain cross cultural experience as well as mission experience. The students, with the assistance of the chaplain's office, raise funds for the mission trip. The chaplain assists in coordinating these trips with the ministry settings on the field. Emphasis is given to the student's opportunity to minister, win friends, and gain knowledge of the particular culture.

Administration:

The chaplain, as part of the college staff, participates fully in the committees and task forces that are required for the functioning of the college. These responsibilities are important to the chaplain's role because they impact the quality of life on the campus and the mission of the school. Bratt continues:

> Seeing the transformational work that God is doing in the lives of college students and having a part in that is a great blessing....I have been able to sit with students who have lost loved ones, students who are preparing for marriage, and students who are trying to discern the next step beyond school. Being a college chaplain places a pastor at the center of this formative time when students are changing radically. My favorite story across the past year was watching a young man who very much connected with and missed the outgoing chaplain, slowly making connections with this new chaplain from whom he sought friendship, direction, theological inquiry, and debate, as well as love and encouragement. By year's end there was a letting down of defenses and a relationship that always begins and ends with a hug. College chaplains can make a difference.

Central Christian College

CENTRAL CHRISTIAN COLLEGE OF MCPHERSON, Kansas, like Roberts Wesleyan, is also associated with the Free Methodist Church. Central came to a position of campus chaplain after trying several other models. The title of the chaplain's position is listed as Dean of Student Development/Campus Pastor. Dr. Leonard Favara, a faculty member, who was involved in the development of this model, reported that in the late 1990s the administration saw the need to assign the responsibility of the students' spiritual development to a particular person. A faculty member was designated Campus Pastor, but this responsibility was an additional duty along with the normal teaching load. Dr. Favara goes on to say that when he arrived on campus in 2000, the administration designated one-quarter of his time to developing a campus ministries office. He was given a student who worked under him as an associate campus pastor or spiritual life director.

The next few years were dedicated to the development and improvement of many of the programs now associated with campus spiritual life such as chapel programs, small groups, missions, etc. Eventually, the duties of a quarter-time campus pastor became too daunting. A search was made for a half time chaplain. Matt Ball was named Campus Pastor and served for one year. In 2008, Chris Smith replaced Ball and now serves in the position.

Other colleges and universities, with which our denomination is associated, employ some form of college chaplain but their titles, their place in the college structure and their position descriptions, vary.

Asbury College

ALTHOUGH NOT A FREE METHODIST college, Asbury College has a large number of Free Methodist students, faculty, and administration members represented on campus. Joy Ireland is a ministerial candidate in the New South Conference and serves in the position of Assistant Chaplain\Assistant Director of Student Ministries. Chaplain Ireland became interested in campus ministry after graduating from Seattle Pacific University. She took a year's internship with the Wesley Foundation at Southern Methodist University in Dallas, Texas. Later, as she was finishing her studies at Asbury Theological Seminary, God made it clear to her that her ministry would be in a non-parish setting. She then applied for a campus chaplain position at Asbury College and was accepted. She has been a college chaplain for four years.

Because Chaplain Ireland's insights into college chaplaincy today are so penetrating, honest and thoughtful, a portion of a paper written by her is included below:

CALLED TO THE CAMPUS
By
Chaplain Joy Ireland

College chaplaincy plays an essential and unique role in modern Christianity. It doesn't take long to consider the dynamics of hundreds, perhaps thousands, of young adults living in close quarters away from home. Questions regarding both present and future flood minds and hearts, and the lessons or coping mechanisms learned in the past are not always the most beneficial tools to bring resolution or peace. Some desire to develop a personal faith separated from their parents. Some have so much baggage due to broken families or traumatic experiences. Some have an extremely strong moral compass or are highly convicted to make a huge impact on their world to the glory of God, but they are not exactly certain about how to hear God's voice clearly. Some struggle with low self-confidence. Some doubt their faith. Some feel the pressures of family expectations. Some deal with a combination of these or other challenges. No matter how strong of a church family these students may encounter on Sunday and/or Wednesday, these issues are loud within them throughout the week.

Pastoral presence on the college campus provides a consistent, safe place to come with deep questions of faith. It is not the only place to come, of course. On Asbury College's campus, support abounds from staff and faculty members in countless areas/departments. However, it is significant for an institution to recognize the importance of hiring a staff whose primary responsibilities revolve around students' overall spiritual nurture and vitality. From intentional thoughts pertaining to chapel themes and speaker scheduling to creating fresh programs that educate and challenge, from preparing and training student leaders for mission experiences to encouraging women (in particular) that God does not uphold the same limits in ministry that they may have experienced or been taught, campus chaplaincy requires a balance as it regards proclaiming foundational truths of the faith in a manner that can be heard and understood by the upcoming generation.

Campus chaplaincy is not a 9am-5pm job. This truth highlights one of the challenges of ministry…life balance. Without proper perspective, it could be quite easy for the campus chaplain to forget the command for Sabbath, though it is a possible temptation for people in other types of ministries. Sabbath observance can be particularly difficult in a campus setting when it is not honored corporately. Campus events are sometimes scheduled on the weekends. Saying no to your boss or employer is difficult. Gratefully, this is not an issue I have had to face often at Asbury College, but I know colleagues who maneuver these waters frequently.

Connected to Sabbath adherence on the job is the balancing act of not getting so heavily involved in the local church setting. This may sound borderline blasphemous coming from one in vocational ministry, but it is a very important lesson God has taught me over my four years in campus chaplaincy. Most local church pastors are able to take a weekday off for their Sabbath observance. However, taking a weekday off is not feasible for the campus chaplain. So much of the academic schedule revolves around the Monday to Friday school week. In fact, there can be so many things to juggle on a given work week, that I often find myself working at least a few hours each Saturday simply to catch up on what didn't get done. Sunday becomes the only day that Sabbath can be observed in a true sense. It is a day of learning and not leading, of hearing the voice of God through teaching and preaching and not being the teacher or preacher. Besides being the right obedient step, it is a deep, personal conviction. I cannot teach students the importance of Sabbath observance if I'm not adhering to it myself. I happen to attend the same church as many Asbury College students, so it is all the more important that action match teaching. The authenticity and integrity of the Gospel is at stake here.

Despite the difficulties associated with personal discipleship and obedience pertaining to Sabbath, campus chaplaincy is extremely rewarding. Perhaps the most satisfying aspect is the opportunity to play a role in a young person's spiritual development. That which is deeply and truly spiritual is never superficial. Being a campus chaplain has opened doors for me to be entrusted with students' significant fears and failures. It has also provided opportunities for me to speak words of encouragement and challenge to men and women regarding their potential in God's kingdom. The privilege of speaking words higher than a student has dared to grasp is humbling. Challenging a student to seriously consider, even grapple with, their commitment to personal and social holiness in a way deeper than their current understanding allows is energizing. Not every student takes the next step, but my success as a chaplain is not measured by their response. It is determined by my willingness and ability to live out the *Great Commission* in the campus context.

Jesus was in the business of meeting people where they were. It is in similar fashion, most often in one-on-one settings, that I find the greatest joy as a campus chaplain, for it is in these situations that my spiritual gifts of shepherding, teaching, and leadership collide. It is also after these scenarios that I sit back and reflect with absolute confidence that I *am* called to the campus. I think of Linda* who sat with me a month ago, glowing with contentment and joy and thanking me for seeing in her what she didn't see in herself or believe God could see in her. Rather than being wracked by low self-esteem and an eating disorder, she now serves in a senior spiritual leadership role on campus. I think of Dennis* who recently came back into town to visit and specifically requested time with me after being away from campus for well over a year. Our last encounter had been quite tough. He desired to thank me for pastoring and caring for him during a time of poor decisions, and he wanted me to know first-hand how God was restoring and healing him. Then there's Rhonda* who invited me into the quandaries and confusion of young love. She sensed a disconnect between her heart for Jesus and the trajectory of a dating relationship and desired sincere pastoral counsel, prayer, and strength regarding a hard decision to be made. Stories like this abound. One person or interaction at a time, I am called to partner with God in making disciples of all nations. And it really takes place! Then these students graduate, covering the globe to do the same. There is absolutely nothing else I'd rather do!

*names changed to protect student identities.

Chaplain Ireland continues to serve with excitement and effectiveness on a growing college campus.

The Uniqueness of the Campus Chaplain

A STUDY OF CAMPUS CHAPLAINS reveals some unique differences between campus chaplains and chaplains in other institutions. One of these differences is that most colleges, both secular and Christian, do not always seem comfortable in giving the title of "Chaplain" to these spiritual leaders. They often use other titles which seem to limit the responsibilities of the position to working only with students rather than including their ministry to the faculty, staff, and this limited role. A third major difference between the campus chaplains and chaplains of other settings, is that most educational institutions do not require that their chaplains be endorsed by a religious body.

Chaplain Jim Ferguson, Brenham State School

A SPECIAL CAMPUS THAT HARDLY fits the stereotypical educational institution has a Free Methodist chaplain assigned to it. Located in Brenham, Texas, Brenham State School is an institution for 700 mentally-challenged persons, in residential and group homes. This unusual school provides care and education to special-needs children and adults, ranging from ages eight to fifty-eight. Providing pastoral care for such a range of ages and their special needs, requires the very highest and best in a chaplain. Chaplain Jim Ferguson is the man God has gifted with the necessary compassion, flexibility, patience, and love for these special people.

On one occasion, at a chaplains' conference, he shared about his work and the challenges he faced in communicating with one particular resident who suffered from a disability in speech and thought. In spite of this almost insurmountable challenge, Chaplain Ferguson developed a deep and trusting relationship with the resident. Ferguson provided the man the support, friendship, and spiritual care he needed to survive and grow. As I heard Chaplain Ferguson tell his moving story, I thought of some pastors I had heard complaining about their difficult church people. I thought to myself, "If they could have walked a mile in the chaplain's shoes at Brenham State School, they would never complain again."

Chaplain Ferguson has found great satisfaction and meaning in bringing Christ to this special campus. After years of challenging and difficult Christ-like service, he is looking forward to retirement. God is no doubt looking for someone else at this moment to fill his shoes. Campus chaplaincy, in the writer's opinion, is one of the richest opportunities available for ministry in a closed community. While recognizing the difficulty involved in financing a chaplain's ministry to secular campuses, it nevertheless offers a rich and fruitful opportunity for those who can find a way. There is certainly room for discussion of this subject in our denomination since our nation's leaders are products of our campuses. If we are to influence our culture, our denomination needs to be represented through chaplains on our college and university campuses.

CONCLUSION

To conclude our study of Free Methodist chaplaincy history, it seems appropriate to make some helpful observations and suggest some areas for further study and research. First, it was overwhelmingly clear to the writer that the Free Methodist chaplains have exceptionally high morale and are doing a difficult but wonderful work on behalf of the Christ and the Church. Few leave the chaplaincy except for retirement or for circumstances beyond their control. In most cases their ministry is extremely demanding and requires a high degree of accountability, yet they gain a high degree of satisfaction in their work. Over all, our chaplains receive the finest training and are involved in continuing-education programs throughout most of their careers. They are thoroughly knowledgeable of other faith groups and can accommodate these needs without compromising their own. In other words, our chaplains are secure enough in their own faith to not be threatened by the beliefs of others.

Our chaplains are also skilled in administration. The institutional setting in which they serve demands that they record and report accurately on the ministry they do and the committees they lead. These records must be of the nature and quality that can stand the close scrutiny of the institutions top leadership, official inspectors, and in some cases, examination by a court of law.

One of the often overlooked critical elements of the chaplaincy is the personal risk chaplains are asked to endure in the course of their duties. It is easy for us to visualize the risk of our military chaplains as they serve with our fighting forces, but equally at risk are the police and firefighter chaplains who accompany law enforcement and firefighters to crime scenes, domestic conflicts, and dangerous fire and rescue operations. The same could be said of our healthcare chaplains who put themselves at risk daily to minister in a contagious environment to the sick and dying; and our correctional chaplains who risk their personal safety by walking and ministering among angry, unstable and dangerous inmates. Our chaplains need the churches' prayers for their daily protection.

In a day when moral failure is a critical issue for clergy in all denominations, the Free Methodist chaplaincy has been remarkable free from this problem. One cannot say that it is because of a lack of opportunity or the chaplain's protected ministry setting. The best answer, in my judgment, is that the chaplains are often held to a stricter standard of accountability by their ministry setting and frequently exposed to training regarding their conduct in counseling and in other high risk relationships.

It is satisfying to report that our chaplains no longer minister in the degree of isolation they once did. As the result of the intentional and outstanding work of the Chaplains Association, the Endorsing Agent/Director of Chaplains, and the strong support of the assigned Bishop (presently Bishop Matthew Thomas) and increasingly that of Conference Supertendents, no chaplain need minister in disassociation from the Church unless they choose to do so. All the structures are now in place to keep the chaplain connected to the Church and the Church connected to the chaplain.

Finally, two areas that are worthy of further study and research:

(1) It is the writer's observation that, although chaplains are very diligent in their ministry assignments, some find it difficult to reflect on or express the rich meaning and depth of what God is doing through and around them. I know I struggled with this when I was a chaplain. How to meet all your responsibilities and still find time for reflection may be one of the chaplain's greatest challenges. There is room for further study at this point.

(2) Finally, because of the Church's early failure to understand and embrace the chaplaincy ministry, I'm certain that we have missed opportunities to realize the mental, emotional and spiritual conflicts that some of our chaplains experienced. To these wounded warriors who bore their battles and pain alone, we offer our sincere apologies and ask their forgiveness. We all bear a responsibility for one another and we all need one another. Although there is always room for improvement, our Church's chaplaincy is alive, well, and growing.

APPENDIXES

SEEKING A CHAPLAIN POSITION

Finding a chaplain position can seem overwhelming; however, there are proven ways to proceed. Here are some helpful hints:

(1) Your Church's Endorsing Agent/Director's office is a good place to begin. This office is often aware of positions that are or will become available. This office needs to know that you are seeking a position.

(2) Institutions often advertise position openings in newspapers, publications and on line.

(3) Military services now have chaplain recruiters who will talk to you about positions and their needs for military chaplains.

(4) To apply for state chaplain positions you should check your state procedures for they vary from state to state. For example, in New York State, the Council of Churches acts as a screening board for all state chaplains.

(5) Pastoral Care Departments at seminaries often have knowledge of chaplain positions.

(6) Chaplains who are already serving in these settings are always good resources for positions that may be available.

(7) One of the most overlooked means of finding a position is to volunteer as a chaplain in the setting of your choice. Often institutions choose their chaplains from the ranks of their volunteers because they have had an opportunity to observe their competency, qualifications and work ethic.

(8) Finally, chaplain professional organizations can also serve to guide you in your search.

Once a position is found, start with your Conference Superintendent. You will need his/her support and approval for your recommendation. The next step is to contact your Church Endorsing Agent who will guide you in your application for endorsement to that particular setting. Endorsement is granted by the Board of Bishops; they then submit a letter of endorsement on your behalf to the institutional setting stating that you are a clergyperson in good standing, qualified to represent your Church to their institution.

ENDORSING AGENTS

Leslie Marston	1941-1962
Robert Crandall	1962-1974
Lawrence Schoenhals	1974-1981
Bruce Kline	1981-1991
Dean Cook	1991-1995
Harry Ansted Jr.	1995-1999
Robert Barnard	1999-2006
Rex Carpenter	2007-

CHAPLAINS ASSOCIATION PRESIDENTS

Randall Tucker	1983-1985
Daniel Hummer	1986-1988
Myron Henry	1988-1990
Dean Cook	1990-1992
Harold Cranston	1992-1994
Harold Hannum	1994-1996
Rex Carpenter	1996-1998
Benjamin Belcher	1998-2000
Imo Smith	2000-2002
James ~~J156~~ Ferguson	2002-2004
Lael Dixon	2004-2006
David Nicholson	2006-2009
Samuel Shreffler	2009-

Adamson, Martin   Air Force   GPL

CHAPLAIN DIRECTORY

MILITARY

NAME	BRANCH OF SERVICE	ANNUAL CONFERENCE*
Ackley, Charles	Navy	PNW
Ailing, Herbert	Army	SMI
Allayaud, William	Army	PIT
Ansted, Harry B., Sr.	Army	PNW
Ansted, Harry B., Jr.	Air Force	PNW
Bailey, Harvey	Army	PNW
Ballew, David	Army	MAM
Barnard, Robert, Jr.	Army	NSC
Beitelshies [Ray], E. R.	Air Force	ARZ
Belcher, Benjamin	Navy	PNW
Bell, Roscoe	Air Force	PNW
Bertholf, Kirby	Army	NMI
Biddulph, George	Army	SCA
Birdsall, Bergen	Army	SCA
Bridges, Donald	Air Force	GEN
Buckley, Gail	Navy	SMI
Burgess, Charles	Air Force	NYK
Cabrera, Samuel	Army	NYK
Carpenter, Kenneth	Army	NSC
Carpenter, Rex	Air Force	GEN
Carroll, Richard	Navy	ORE
Carter, Herstel	Navy	NSC
Coates, Stephen	Navy	GAT
Cook, E. Dean	Navy	ORE

Dollar, Ernest	Navy	GPL
Darling, A. W.	Army	CRV
Demond, Dennis	Army	NMI
Fero, Francis	Army	SPC
Fristo, Kenneth	Army	SPC
Gifford, Clayton	Army	NSC
Grizzard, Mark	Air Force	ALG
Hannum, Harold	Army	NCC
Harford, Alva	Army	WAB
Hawley, Leon	Army	CRV
Hayes, Robert	Army	ORE
Henry, Myron	Navy	GAT
Herndon, Bart	Army	MAM
Holderman, Gary	Army	GPL
Holliday, James	Army	CRV
Hoyt, John	Air Force	SAC
Hubbs, John	Army	GAT
Jones, Terry	Army	SAC
Klein, Robert	Army	GAT
Leach, Raymond	Army	NCC
Legg II, Robert	Air Force	PNW
Mack, Walter	Army	PNW
Mallory, Charles	Air Force	NCC
Martin, Kim	Air Force	EMI
Mayhew, Kendall	Army	GAT
Mitchener, Michael	Navy	GAT
Mullett, Owen	Army	GAT
Ogden, Horatio	Army	CRV
Pahs, David	Navy	RMT
Peters, Charles	Air Force	GAT
Porter, Oliver	Army	NCC
Porter, Timothy	Air Force	ORE
Probst, Merlin	Army	OHO

Racster, Larry	Army	WAB
Randall, Anthony	Army	RMT
Ray [Beitelshies], E. R.	Air Force	ARZ
Reber, Carson	Army	GEN
Robb, Wesley	Navy	SCA
Rohrer, Clason	Air Force	SPC
Ronne, Lowell	Air Force	SPC
Roots, Charles	Navy	SPC
Schwab, Samuel	Navy	PNW
Smith, Imo	Army	PNW
Smith, William	Army (Canada)	PNW
Spond, Kurt	Army	NSC
Stanton, Robert	Army	PNW
Sweezy, Dwight	Army	NYK
Thompson, David	Navy	NCC
Thornton, Leo	Army	ORE
Timm, Harry	Army	PNW
Toney, Victor	Air Force	OHO
Trudgen, William	Army	MDV
Tucker, Randall	Army	NSC
Tugan, Gary	Navy	SAC
Walls, Forest	Army	PNW
Warren, Robert	Army	MDV
Webb, Harry	Army	OHO
Whiteman, George	Army	SCA
Williams, Mark	Air Force	SAC
Wilson, Jack	Army	NCC
Wilson, Steve	Army	NRV
Winchester, Richard	Army	NSC
Woods, C. E.	Air Force	MDV
Worthley, W.	Army	CRC
Wright, Jon	Army	SPC
Zimmerman, Donald	Air Force	ARZ

CIVIL AIR PATROL

NAME	ANNUAL CONFERENCE
Hend, Everett	GPN
Magee, Robert	MDV
Martin, Kim	EMI
McLaughlin, D. P.	SCA
Russell, Mervin	WAB
Smith, David	SCA
Warde, Vincent	SPC
Watson, Claude	SCA

HOSPITAL

Bahena, Marilyn	SMI
Baird, Ronald	CRV
Bastien, Ed	OHO
Belcher, Benjamin	PNW
Bishop, Harold	MAM
Burleigh, Douglas	NYK
Cartrette, Philip	GUL
Casurella, H	NSC
Channel, Norman	OHO
Coleman, Cherlyn	SCA
Cranston, Harold	MAM
Deighton, Donald	OHO
Furgeson, James	TEX
Fry, Timothy	GAT
Gates, Godfrey	KEY
Jackson, Mary	SMI
Lehman, Howard	MAM
McIntyre, Wesley	ORE
Meyers, Vincent	SMI

Miers, Ronald	GPL
Olver, Harold	NYK
Shinabarger, Delbert	NCC
Smith, William	CRV
Snell, Brian	GPL
Sweezy, Dwight	NYK

VETERANS ADMINISTRATION

Dixon, Lael	WAB
Hummer, Daniel	SAC
McLaren, Rob	SAC
Roller, Raymond	ARZ
Schantz, Paul	NSC
Swingle, Bruce	NEC
Taylor, Larry	ORE
Tucker, Randall	ARZ
Webb, Harry	SMI
Wright, Jon	SPC

HOSPICE

Demaray, James	NSC
Hall, Daleasha	ORE
Munoz, Diane	NSC
Simpson, Fletcher	NCC
Stevenson, Melvin	EMI

CORRECTIONS

Ball, David	GUL
Beers, Jeanne	KEY
Carney, Boyd	PIT
Demond, Dennis	NMI

Fry, Timothy	GAT
Hallock, John	ORE
Henry, Myron	GAT
Holman, Thomas	SAC
Iske, Richard	GPN
Kantonen, Lee	NSC
Lowery, William, Sr.	GEN
Martinez, Joseph	PNW
Mogenson, Christopher	NYK
Reitz, Debra	KEY
Smith, Eric	TEX
Smith, Imo	PNW
Vecchiarelli, Linda	RMT

RETIREMENT COMMUNITIES

Demond, Dennis	NMI
Dey, Virgil	GEN
Dodge, Wesley	PNW
Lattimer, Paul	NSC
McGinnis, Raymond	GEN
Miers, Ronald	GPN
Shreffler, Samuel	GEN
Tjepkema, Mark	ARZ
Vogel, Douglas	WAB

POLICE AND FIREFIGHTERS

Bailey, Robert	SMI
Bradley, Mearl	SMI
Channel, Norman	NCC
Clegg, Daniel	WAB
Harold, James	WAB
Johnson, Wally	ORE

Kincaid, Burton	NMI
Lefler, John	WAB
Mettsinger, David	GEN
Nicholson, David	WAB
Owen, John	GEN

CAMPUS

Bratt, Jonathan	SMI
Cook, Dean	NSC
Cullum, Douglas	GEN
Ferguson, James	TEX
Gaffner, Lori	GAT
Ireland, Joy	NSC
Kilburn, Thomas	GEN
Kopicko, Ronald	SMI
Smith, Christopher	GAT

OTHER

Barnard, Robert	Race Track	NSC
Fuller, Lynn	Tuskegee Airmen	NSC
Reynolds, Richard	Operation Nightwatch	PNW

*ANNUAL CONFERENCE DESIGNATIONS

Arizona	ARZ
Columbia River	CRV
East Michigan	EMI
Gateway	GAT
Genesis	GEN
Great Plains	GPL
Gulf Coast	GUL
Keystone	KEY

Maryland-Virginia	MDV
Mid-America	MAM
New England	NEC
New South	NSC
New York	NYK
North Central	NCC
North Michigan	NMI
Ohio	OHO
Oregon	ORE
Pacific Coast Japanese	PCJ
Pacific Northwest	PNW
Pittsburgh	PIT
Rocky Mountain	RMT
Sierra Pacific	SPC
South Atlantic	SAC
Southern California	SCA
Southern Michigan	SMI
Texas	TEX
Wabash	WAB

Note: All directory designations use the conference titles of 2009

CHAPLAIN PROFESSIONAL ORGANIZATIONS

NACMAF --------National Conference on Ministry to the Armed Forces

COMISS-----------Council on Ministry In Specialized Settings

ACPE ---------------Association of Clinical Pastoral Education

ACCA ---------------American Correctional Chaplain's Association

APC ----------------Association of Professional Chaplains

AAPC ---------------American Association of Pastoral Counselors

AACC---------------American Association of Christian Counselors

ICPC ---------------International Conference of Police Chaplains

ACC ----------------Association of College Chaplains

SELECTED BIBLIOGRAPHY

Beckford, James and Sophie Gilliant. <u>Religion in Prison: Equal Rights in a Multi-Faith Society.</u> Cambridge, Eng.: University Press, 1998.

Benjestorf, G.L. The Chaplain's Role in Critical Incident Response. An overview. In J. T. Reese and H.A. Goldstein (Eds.), <u>Psychological Services for Law Enforcement</u> (pp.111-114). Washington, DC: U.S. Government Printing Office, 1991.

Boozer, Jack S. <u>Edge of Ministry, the Chaplain's Story, U.M. Board of Higher Education and the Ministry.</u> Nashville, TN: Parthenon Press, 1984.

Brummett, Barbara. <u>The Spiritual Campus, The Chaplain and the College Community.</u> Pilgrim Press, 1990.

Chesterton, Sharon and Robert Wicks (Eds.). <u>Essentials of Chaplains</u>. Paulist Press.

Colson, Charles and Daniel Van Ness, <u>Converted, New Yope for Ending America's Crime Crisis.</u> Crossway Books, 1989.

Cook, E. Dean. <u>Salt of the Sea</u>. Longwood, FL: Xulon Publishers, 2006.

Cox, Harvey (Ed.). <u>Military Chaplains: From a Religious Military to a Military Religion.</u> New York: American Report Press, 1973.

Dent, James A. <u>Historical Sketches of Chaplains in the Commonwealth of Kentucky.</u> Federal Prisons, 1971

De Revere, David W, Wilbert Cunningham, Tom Mobly, and John Price. <u>Chaplaincy in Law Enforcement.</u> Charles Thomas Publishers, 1989.

Fisher, C. Some Techniques and External Programs Useful in Police Psychological Services. In J.T. Reese and H.A. Goldstein (Eds.), <u>Psychological Services for Law Enforcement</u> (pp. 111-114). Washington, D.C.: U.S. Government Printing Office, 1986.

Goldstein, H.A. Police Psychology: Influencing Organizational Character in J. T. Reese and J.M. Horn (Eds.), <u>Police Psychology: Operational Assistance</u> (pp. 173-180). Washington, DC: FBI, 1988.

Hadley, Donald and Gerald Richards. <u>Ministry with the Military, A Guide for Churches and Chaplains.</u> Baker Book House, 1991.

Hammond, Philip. <u>Campus Clergy.</u> Basic Books, 1969.

Holst, Lawrence (Ed.). <u>Hospital Chaplaincy, The Role of the Chaplain Today.</u> Thomas Publishers, 1973.

-----and Harold Kurtz (Eds.). <u>Forward, A Creative Chaplaincy.</u> Thomas, 1973.

Kasper, Donald. <u>On Duty: Purpose and Practices in Christian Correctional Chaplains.</u> Longwood, FL: Xulon Press, 2006.

Kroes, W. H. and J. J. Hurrell (Eds.). <u>Job Stress and the Police Officer.</u> Washington, D.C.:U.S. Department of Health, Education and Welfare.

Logan, James S. <u>Good Punishment.</u> William Erdmans, 2008.

Monahan, Luke and Caroline Renekan. <u>The Chaplains, A Faith Presence in the School Community.</u> Columbia Press, 1998.

Paget, Naomi K. and Janet R. McCormick. <u>The Work of the Chaplain.</u> Valley Forge, PA: Judson Press, 2006.

Pennington, Robert. <u>The Christ Chaplain, The Way to a Deeper, More Effective Hospital Ministry.</u> Haworth Pastoral Press, 2007.

<u>Prisons, A Study in Volnurability.</u> Collection of Essays by the Board of Social Responsibility Of the Church of England. London, Eng.: Church House Publishers, 1999.

Shaw, Richard. <u>Chaplains to Imprisoned.</u> New York: Haworth Press, 1995.

Soering, Jens. <u>The Convict Christ, What the Gospel Says About Criminal Justice</u>. Orbis Books, 2006.

Swanson, Edward L. <u>Ministry to the Armed Forces</u>. General Commission on Chaplaincy And Armed Forces Personnel, 1968.

Tenbrook, Gretchen W. <u>Broken Bodies, healing hearts; Reflections of a Hospital Chaplain.</u> New York: Hawthorne Pastoral Press, 2000.

Thompson, David and Darlene Witterstrom. <u>Beyond the Yellow Ribbon: Ministry to Returning Combat Veterans.</u> Abingdon Press, 2009.

Toole, Mary M. <u>Handbook for Chaplains, Comfort My People</u>. Paulist Press, 2006.

Underwood, Kenneth W. <u>The Professional Identity of a Campus Pastor, A Danforth Study of Campus Ministries</u>. Middleton, CN: Wesleyan University Press, 1969.

Ward, David and Gene Kossebaum. <u>Women Prisons, Sexual Social Structure</u>. Aldine Publishers, 1965.

Weise, Carl and David Friar. <u>Terror in the Prisons.</u> Indianapolis, IN: The Bobbs-Merril Co., 1974.

White, Stephen. <u>College Chaplain: A Practical Guide to Campus Ministry.</u> Cleveland: Pilgrim Press, 2005.

LaVergne, TN USA
14 July 2010
189399LV00004B/3/P